GRAND ILLUSIONS

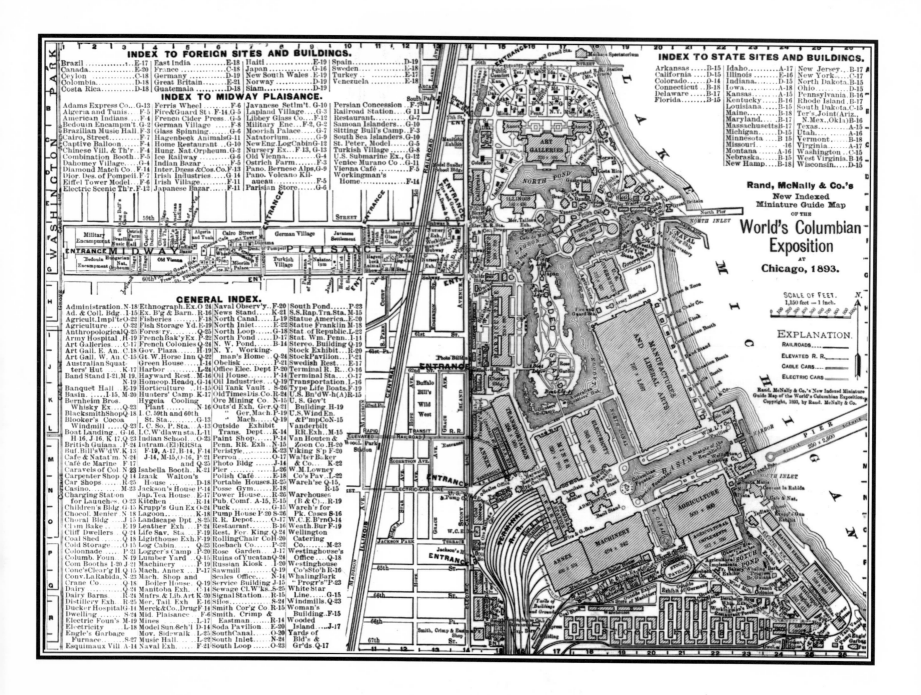

GRAND ILLUSIONS
CHICAGO'S WORLD'S FAIR OF 1893

Neil Harris, Wim de Wit,
James Gilbert, and Robert W. Rydell

Chicago Historical Society

The exhibition *Grand Illusions: Chicago's World's Fair of* 1893 was on view at the Chicago Historical Society from May 1, 1993 to July 17, 1994.

Published in the United States of America in 1993 by the Chicago Historical Society.

Acting Director of Publications, Chicago Historical Society: Claudia Lamm Wood

Edited by Claudia Lamm Wood, Patricia Bereck Weikersheimer, and Rosemary Adams.

Designed by Bill Van Nimwegen.

Composed in Benguiat Condensed, Tiffany, and Novarese. Art produced on a Macintosh IIci with Quark Xpress, Adobe Illustrator, and Adobe Photoshop.

Printed by Great Lakes Graphics, Inc., Skokie, Illinois.

Library of Congress Catalog Card Number: 93-71298.

ISBN 0-913820-18-0

Cover: *The Agriculture Building*, painting by Childe Hassam.

Frontispiece: A souvenir map of the World's Columbian Exposition, published by Rand McNally.

For

Andrew F. Leo, 1949–93

Director of Design

Chicago Historical Society

CONTENTS

LENDERS AND DONORS OF ARTIFACTS

American Ceramic Society Museum

Anheuser-Busch Companies, Inc.

Armour Food Co.

Art Institute of Chicago, Burnham Library

Art Institute of Chicago, Department of Imaging
and Technical Services

Florence Baughman

Borden, Inc.

The Brooklyn Museum,
R. B. Woodward Memorial Fund

Brooklyn Public Library, Brooklyn Collection

Buffalo Bill Historical Center

City of Minneapolis, Records Archives Division

Cleveland Public Library

Continental Bank

Deere & Company

Denver Public Library,
Western History Department

Paul Dettloff, D.V. M.

Larry Dixon

Downers Grove Historical Museum

Linda Fess

Field Museum of Natural History

Henry Ford Museum & Greenfield Village

Steve Frank

Doug Fymbo

Karen Gagen

General Mills, Inc. Archives

Michael Gustafson/Collectors Series

Mrs. Carol Jo Heald

Mr. and Mrs. Harlow Niles Higinbotham

Gregory Jorjorian

Frank J. Katlin

Lawrence Public Library

Thomas J. Lipton Co.

Kevin Lynch

Massachusetts Institute of Technology Museum

William Hammond Mathers Museum

Frank D. Mayer, Jr.

Minnesota Historical Society

Museum of History and Industry

Nabisco Brands Inc.

The Newberry Library

The New-York Historical Society

Northwestern University Library,
Special Collections

Pabst Brewing Co.

Peabody Museum of Archaeology
and Anthropology

Cliff Peterson Collection

Port of History Museum

Public Museum of Grand Rapids

Quaker Oats Co.

Hazel E. Robinson

Salvage One

Smithsonian Institution,
Division of Electricity and Modern Physics

State Historical Society of Iowa, Museum Bureau

State Historical Society of Wisconsin

The Stroh Brewing Co.

University Museum of Archaeology
and Anthropology

Donors

The exhibition *Grand Illusions: Chicago's World's Fair of* 1893
was made possible in part through the generosity of:

The National Endowment for the Humanities, a federal agency

The Illinois Humanities Council and the Illinois General Assembly

with additional support from:

The Berghoff Restaurant

Editel–Chicago

Sandoz Agro, Inc.

PREFACE

Russell Lewis

Paraphrasing that which Byron wrote of love," commented George Auguste Sala, the noted nineteenth-century writer and traveler about the difference between British and French expositions, "it may be said that the Great Exhibition was of London life only a part, it is Paris' whole existence."[1] Indeed, Paris hosted a record five international expositions between 1855 and 1900. Under French stewardship, world's fairs became identified with cosmopolitanism and, as part of Napoleon III and Baron Haussmann's dramatic transformation of Paris in the 1850s and 1860s, with the rise of the modern city. Although numerous cities hosted fairs in the last half of the nineteenth century—Moscow, Vienna, Calcutta, Budapest, Geneva, New Orleans, Omaha, and Atlanta—Chicago's World's Columbian Exposition was the only one to rival the grandeur of Parisian fairs and to make a lasting contribution to the progress of cities.

The Columbian Exposition strengthened the identification of world's fairs with the evolution of cities. In its vast scale, the Chicago exposition's 633 acres of fairgrounds dwarfed previous Parisian expositions. Indeed, the Chicago fair, popularly known as the White City, was the first to be compared to an ideal city. For noted Universalist minister John Coleman Adams, it was a city that was "orderly and convenient. . . . Nothing in any of the exhibits within the walls of these great buildings," he wrote, "was half so interesting, so suggestive, so full of hopeful intonations, as the Fair in its aspects as a city by itself. In the midst of a very real and very earthy city, full of the faults which Chicago so preeminently displays, we saw a great many features of what an ideal city might be, a great many visions which perhaps will one day become solid facts, and so we moved the blot and failure of modern civilization, the great city at the end of the century."[2] For Robin and Meg Macleod, the waifs in Francis Hodgson Burnett's allegory, *Two Little Pilgrim's Progress*, the exposition was the "City Beautiful,"[3] and for Samantha, the heroine of Marietta Holley's novel about the world's fair, the White City was the "New Jerusalem."[4] Journalist Richard Harding Davis wrote of the fair, "This is a really great

Crowds of people filled the fairgrounds for the Chicago Day celebration, held on October 9, 1893, to commemorate the anniversary of the Great Chicago Fire of 1871.

city—in its way, the conception and carrying out of the laws of this municipality is one of the most wonderful features of the fair."[5]

But the contrast drawn between the fair and Chicago, between the White City and the gray city, was not nearly as dramatic as these fair observers or contemporary scholars would have us believe. Although the exposition projected a powerful and compelling image of harmony, unity, and beauty, it was a masterful illusion; upon closer examination the fair also reveals that the nation's prejudices and

exclusionary practices were incorporated into the planning, building, and running of the exposition. Rather than celebrating the diversity of American society and the varied cultures of the world, the Columbian Exposition, like other world's fairs before it, presented a calculated division of the world into civilized and primitive realms. Women, African-Americans, Native Americans, and so-called "exotic" peoples from around the world were either excluded from participating in the fair or confined to specific pavilions, exhibits, or Midway attractions. The White City, like its host city, was a product of struggle and controversy. This counterpoint of fair themes—the significant cultural achievements and accompanying visions of grandeur on the one hand and the conflicts and the contested issues shaping Chicago and America's growing urban society on the other—is the focus of the exhibition *Grand Illusions: Chicago's World's Fair of 1893* and this catalogue.

The World's Columbian Exposition was built under the direction of one man, Daniel Burnham. While everyone has always been impressed by Burnham's leading role, it becomes even more impressive when one considers that an exhibition about the fair could only be organized through a team process in which numerous people worked together to realize the project. And yet in every team there emerges a Burnham-like figure whose vision and energy create an atmosphere and set a pace within which the project unfolds. Wim de Wit, curator of the Society's Charles F. Murphy Architectural Center, played this pivotal role for the *Grand Illusions* team. As curator of the exhibition, he developed the conceptual framework for interpreting the fair, and he was involved in every aspect of its planning and execution. Without his commitment and dedication over many years, his unbridled enthusiasm for the project, his patience in the face of problems and delays, and his willingness to share unselfishly with staff members the joys of curatorial work, *Grand Illusions* could not have been realized on such a large and comprehensive scale.

Neil Harris, Preston and Sterling Morton Professor of History at the University of Chicago, also deserves special thanks for his many insightful contributions to the project during the development of the conceptual framework. In his capacity as special historical consultant to the exhibition, he skillfully guided the exhibition planners to focus on the theme of contest, and thus he placed an indelible stamp on the exhibition. Susan Page Tillett, the Society's director of curatorial affairs and project director for *Grand Illusions* until August 1, 1992, also played an indispensable role in the formulation of the exhibition. Susan first suggested organizing an exhibition about the World's Columbian Exposition, and her enthusiastic support of the project until she left the Society (and even after) helped keep it on a steady course. In her role as research assistant, Connie Casey managed the day-to-day work of the exhibition with efficiency and good cheer. Her responsibilities expanded greatly as her knowledge of the fair's history and her curatorial insights became essential to completing the exhibition. An ideal partner for Wim, she developed the thematic interpretation and selected the artifacts for two sections of the exhibition.

and concepts. Joining Neil Harris were James Gilbert, University of Maryland at College Park; Helen L. Horowitz, Smith College; Michael Leja, Northwestern University; Robert Rydell, Montana State University; and Alan Trachtenberg, Yale University. Each brought a different perspective to the discussions, and their advice helped us to focus the ideas of the exhibition more clearly. Some of their insights are developed in the chapters of this catalogue; we are fortunate to have contributions by Neil Harris, James Gilbert, and Robert Rydell.

The staff of the Chicago Historical Society provided immeasurable support and assistance, and for all their help I am truly appreciative. I am very grateful to the Society's former president and director, Ellsworth H. Brown, for his support throughout all phases of the exhibition. Collections manager Mike Sarna imposed the highest professional standards in his management of the shipping, storage, and tracking of artifacts. Joanne Grossman, special projects manager, provided welcome administrative talents to many different aspects of the exhibition. Wendy Greenhouse, former curator of paintings and sculpture, provided assistance in developing the planning grant.

The design office did a masterful job of transforming ideas and themes on paper into a three-dimensional experience for visitors to enjoy. We were extremely saddened by the death of director of design Andrew Leo earlier this year. Andy played a crucial role in the team process, and his extraordinary sense of design is evident in every part of *Grand Illusions*. The exhibition and this catalogue are dedicated to his memory. His partner in designing the exhibition, Michael Biddle, who assumed the position of director of design, supervised the final

*Randolph Street looking east
from LaSalle Street, 1892.
Photograph by J. W. Taylor.*

Mechanized attractions, such as the Ferris Wheel, above, and the Moving Sidewalk, opposite, were among the most popular novelties of the fair.

stages of constructing and installing one of the most spectacular shows ever mounted at the Chicago Historical Society. Bill Van Nimwegen provided compelling graphic designs for this catalogue, street banners, invitations, and exhibition labels; he was ably assisted by Ted Gibbs. Preparators Wally Reinhardt and Myron Freedman and their crews of talented carpenters, painters, and installers did a remarkable job of recreating the scale of the fair and building a seamless exhibition for visitors to enjoy. Myron's vision of the dramatic role video can play in a museum setting is evident in the stunning multimedia production that he supervised and which is shown in the transformed North Atrium.

The publications office staff brought order and clarity to the exhibition catalogue and labels. Claudia Lamm Wood, acting director of publications, Rosemary Adams, assistant editor, and former assistant editor Patricia Bereck Weikersheimer patiently read and critiqued numerous drafts of catalogue and label copy. The final results are greatly improved because of their efforts. Interns Susan Boothe, Lydia Field, Nicholas Suh, and publications assistant Robert K. Parker III made invaluable contributions to the editing process.

Bonnie Garmisa, associate educator, strongly advocated making the exhibition more accessible to visitors in the many discussions about learning objectives and design concepts that took place. Thanks to her input, the scholarly themes were translated into an exhibition that will have broad public appeal. The school and public programs developed by Bonnie, Amina Dickerson, director of education, Lynn McRainey, associate educator, and the Cheney Center staff will further interpret the story of the fair told in the exhibition.

John Alderson, photographer, and Jay Crawford, assistant photographer, produced all the photographs for both the exhibition and the catalogue; they completed this enormous volume of work in a timely fashion, ensuring the highest technical and professional standards for each image.

David Gillingham, vice president of development, Sue Devine, director of development, and Leslie Wygert, manager of the annual fund, managed the fundraising effort for the exhibition. Laura Lacchia, membership manager, organized the events for the exhibition opening. Pat Kremer, public relations manager, pursued the media relentlessly and insured that word of the exhibition would reach a broad public.

Many staff members in the Society's curatorial departments helped locate objects and provided information for the exhibition. Their contributions were essential to the success of our exhibition. I want to thank Larry Viskochil, Linda Ziemer, Eileen Flanagan, Diane Ryan, and Claire Cass of the prints and photographs department; Sarah Carey of the department of decorative and industrial arts; Janice McNeill and Emily Clark of the library; Barbara Schreier and Gayle Strege of the costume collection; Archie Motley, archives and manuscripts; and Riva Feschbach, former assistant curator of paintings and sculpture. I also want to thank Carol Turchan and Nancy Buenger, the Society's paper and costume conservators, as well as volunteers Roberta Hotzel, Helena Kagestedt, Fredi Lecof, and Phyliss Willett in the costume conservation lab. Christine del Re and Mark Hayward conserved many three-dimensional objects in the exhibition.

We were lucky enough to find many interns and volunteers who helped us with our research. Thom

Collins, Willa Cramton, Sara Doris, Pam Harkins, Katie Horazy, Amy Mooney, Niven Q. Reily, George Sargeant, Lena Tramonte, and Max Zavitz provided critical support during the planning and implementation phases.

During the organization of the exhibition we also received advice from many specialists outside the Chicago Historical Society. We want to thank the following individuals for their willingness to answer our questions and locate objects for the exhibition: William Gates, American Ceramic Society Museum; Mary Louise Brown, Anheuser Busch Companies, Inc.; Jan R. Brandstetter, Armour Food Corporation; Luigi Mumford, Mary Woolever, and Lieschen A. Potuznik, The Art Institute of Chicago; Dovie Patrick and Wilson Flemister, Robert W. Woodruff Library, Atlanta University Center; Robert G. Benz, Billings Farm and Museum; Janet Houghton, Billings Mansion Archives; Jeanne Washko, Borden, Inc.; Barbara Dayer Gallati, Kathleen Flynn, Deirdre Lawrence, and Deborah Wythe, The Brooklyn Museum; Judith Walsh, Brooklyn Public Library; Elizabeth Smith Buckles; Joanne Kudla and Paul Fees, Buffalo Bill Historical Center; Andrew Bullen, Center for Research Libraries; Bart Ryckbosch, Chicago Park District; Earl Gerding and Kirk Kekatos, Chicago Photographic Collectors Society; Alice Loranth, Cleveland Public Library; Janet Parks, Avery Architectural and Fine Arts Library, Columbia University; Allen Serbus, Continental Bank; Les Stegh, Deere & Company; Karen Dekker; Susan Edwards, Denver Parks and Recreation Planning Department; Carol B. Spitler, Downers Grove Historical Museum; Todd Gustavson, George Eastman House; Suzanne Epstein; Linda Fess; Christine Gross, William Grewe-Mullins, and Janice B. Klein, Field Museum of Natural

History; Peter H. Cousins and Clara Deck, Henry Ford Museum and Greenfield Village; Jean Toll, General Mills, Inc.; Mrs. Carol Jo Heald; Mr. and Mrs. Harlow Niles Higinbotham; Joseph Dionne, Lawrence Public Library; Mary F. Pfeil, Thomas J. Lipton Co.; Kevin Lynch; Lois Markus; Kara Schneiderman, Massachusetts Institute of Technology Museum; Elizabeth Cook, William Hammond Mathers Museum; Karen Lovaas, Minnesota Historical Society; Rick Caldwell, Museum of History and Industry; David R. Stivers, Nabisco Brands, Inc.; Mary Porter

Wyly, The Newberry Library; Mary Beth Betts and Karen Waldemar, The New-York Historical Society; Emily A. Nixon, Nixon Art Associates; Patrick Quinn, Northwestern University Archives; R. Russell Maylone, Northwestern University Library Special Collections; John Steiner, Pabst Brewing Co.; Genevieve Fisher and Gloria Greis, Peabody Museum of Archaeology and Anthropology; Corliss Cavalieri, Port of History Museum; Marilyn Merdzinski, Public Museum of Grand Rapids; Janet Rankaitis, Quaker Oats Co.; Terry Sharrar and Shawn Johnstone, Smithsonian Institution; Jodene K. Evans, State Historical Society of Iowa, Museum Bureau; Paul G. Bourcier and Carol Larsen, State Historical Society of Wisconsin; Tom Appel, Studebaker National Museum; Jonas Stundza; Jennifer Mathison, Swedish-American Association of Chicago; Jennifer L. White, Lucy F. Williams, and Sylvia Smith, University Museum of Archaeology and Anthropology.

Finally, I want to thank the following colleagues from other Chicago institutions who agreed to coordinate events with us to celebrate the centennial of the World's Columbian Exposition: Mary Woolever and Susan Godlewski, The Art Institute of Chicago; Sally Hess and Bill Hinchliff, Chicago Architecture Foundation; Andrea Mark, Harold Washington Public Library; Alexia Trzyna, Field Museum; Sue Eleuterio, Museum of Science and Industry; and Mary Beth Herr and Janet Smith of Department of Cultural Affairs of the City of Chicago.

When *Grand Illusions: Chicago's World Fair of* 1893 opens on May 1, 1993, exactly one hundred years after the gates of the White City opened to the world, the future of world's fairs will remain uncertain. Contemporary critics have argued that world's fairs are anachronisms, relics of the past century that have outlived their usefulness in a world bound more closely through sophisticated communication and transportation technology. Chicago's failed attempt to secure a world's fair for the city in 1992 and the less than enthusiastic response to the various fairs of the past decade offer support for this point of view. But if the future of world's fairs is unclear, their legacy is not. They teach us much not only about the people who created them, but also about our own time. Indeed, the story of the spectacular achievements of the Columbian Exposition and the cost of that victory in terms of who lost and who was excluded asks us to consider our own successes and our own sense of progress in a similar light. It is in this spirit of broadening our city's history and of making it meaningful to our nation's diverse citizens that *Grand Illusions: Chicago's World's Fair of* 1893 was created.

NOTES

1. George Augusta Sala, *Paris Herself Again in* 1878–9, vol. II (London: Remington & Co., 1880), 33.

2. John Coleman Adams, "What a Great City Might Be—A Lesson from the White City," *New England Magazine* n.s. 14 (March 1896), 3.

3. Frances Hodgson Burnett, *The Little Pilgrim's Progress* (New York: Scribner's, 1895), 183.

4. Marietta Holley, *Samantha at the World's Fair* (New York: Funk & Wagnalls, 1893), 235.

5. Julian Ralph, "A Recent Journey through the West IX—Chicago since the Fair," *Harper's Weekly* 39 (November 16, 1895), 1088.

MEMORY AND THE WHITE CITY

MEMORY AND THE WHITE CITY

by Neil Harris

Manufactures and Liberal
Arts Building, viewed across
the Grand Basin. Photo-
graph by C. D. Arnold,
official photographer of
the World's Columbian
Exposition.

Few American experiences ever received, at the time they occurred, the intense coverage and careful scrutiny accorded Chicago's World's Columbian Exposition. The brilliantly inventive and comprehensive advertising direction by Moses P. Handy, including an almost unending stream of stories and stunts and a newsletter printed in fourteen languages, ensured continuous attention from journalists. Participating corporations and institutions developed their own publicity materials. Railroads, hotels, and travel agents distributed maps and circulars. And the enormous success the fair enjoyed in attracting millions of visitors made it certain that magazines, newspapers, artists, and writers would devote themselves to describing and analyzing the extravaganza while it was open. The fair's obvious importance forced almost anyone who fancied himself or herself an observer of contemporary mores to visit Chicago for a closer look. Until late 1893 the buildings, special events, celebrity visitors, crowds, and above all, the bustling host city, excited a stream of colorful commentaries that quickly found their way into print.

And then, not unexpectedly but abruptly nonetheless, the fair was over. Not only did it end, but fires, vandalism, and systematic disassembly quickly dismantled almost every physical vestige of its existence. A few ruins managed a fitful life, and there was some adaptive reuse in the Field Columbian Museum.[1] But in later years, a relandscaped Jackson Park and Midway Plaisance—trees planted, the water for the Court of Honor filled in, marinas, golf courses, tennis courts, and bridle paths created for public use—obscured even the outlines of what had been so amazing a national experience. Today's visitors must be guided carefully around the park to gain any sense of the fair's immense scale and complex footprint.

Fairgoers had a sense of evanescence even during the height of the exposition. The dream metaphors so easily applied to the White City suggested not only its magical and illusionistic qualities, but also an awareness that it all would soon vanish, that its pomp and beauty were the things of just a day. Everyone knew that the fairgrounds would not be maintained, that Jackson Park would be returned to the South Park system with the exposition palaces taken down after the closing date. These were normal exposition procedures, and most of the buildings lacked any provisions for permanence.

*Guidebooks and souvenir
programs, right, provided
a way for fairgoers to anti-
cipate and then to remember
the wonders of the World's
Columbian Exposition.
The White City rose as if
by magic from swampland
in Jackson Park, opposite.
The construction site of the
Manufactures and Liberal
Arts Building as it appeared
on October 6, 1891 (top,
looking northeast; bottom,
looking northwest). Photographs by C. D. Arnold.*

the fair's essence for permanent evocation. Aware of the White City's brevity, many visitors responded with urgency to the challenge of remembering it. Photography, becoming steadily more convenient and less expensive, could produce more faithfully detailed records of such scenes than had ever before been possible. Fair officials, with their careful choice of official photographers and licenses for the cameras of individual visitors, acknowledged just how critical the control of images actually was.[2] The exposition grounds, like an exquisite young patient doomed to a fatal and quick-acting disease, had just six months to be savored. And then enthusiastic witnesses would be left with only their memories, souvenirs, and pictures.

The succeeding century endowed the exposition's memory and standing with a life of their own. The excitement of relating to this great event while it was still green and vigorous was followed by a period of intellectual hostility, and then one of casual indifference, before collectors, planners, politicians, artists, architects, and historians would take it up again, to stage new contests over its meaning in the 1970s, 1980s, and 1990s. As we celebrate the fair's one-hundredth birthday, it is useful to examine the shifting status of its reputation, the fickle and erratic chorus that has accompanied its evocations. The character of collective memory, some argue, is performative and socially constructed; it is largely, in the words of Lewis Coser, "a reconstruction of the past in the light of the present."[3] In a changing America it was only natural that the exposition's status should change also, and that the fair be used to legitimate or challenge a wide range of practices and institutions.

But physical evanescence now coexisted with more ambitious demands on collective memory. Various new techniques could capture and preserve

The construction of the Administration Building, opposite, was documented by C. D. Arnold on May 21, 1892.

Left, the completed edifice one year later. Photographs by C. D. Arnold.

The White City vanished more quickly than it had appeared. Fires destroyed many of the buildings. The magnificent Court of Honor was reduced to rubble.

Below, the Statue of the Republic by Daniel Chester French remained as a poignant reminder of the summer of 1893.

Souvenir postcards found their way into scrapbooks and keepsake collections. Views of the buildings as well as of famous persons associated with the World's Columbian Exposition kept alive this influential event in the nation's collective memory.

The first phase of the World's Columbian reputation, the Era of Active Memory, flourished from the closing of the exposition until the 1920s. Many of the more than twelve million visitors remained alive and active; their souvenirs, scrapbooks, postcards and photographs trophies of what remained, decades later, their most memorable adventure.[4] In thousands of parlors the knickknack cabinets beloved by that generation continued to display the innumerable objects— fans, tiny Liberty Bells, Libbey glass miniatures, spoons, ashtrays, bookends, salt and pepper shakers, cups and saucers— contrived for the fair.[5]

The Columbian Exposition's memory was nurtured not only by visitor recall but by the physical existence of half a dozen major international expositions hosted by America in these decades, several of them—in Omaha (1898), Buffalo (1901), St. Louis (1904), Portland (1905), Seattle (1909), San Francisco (1915)—bearing startling resemblances in overall planning and building style to the White City.[6] Their Pikes and Strands and Joy Zones seemed to repeat, in one form or another, the spectacular Midway; indeed concessionaires traveled from one exposition to another, setting up permanent quarters in the urban amusement areas, such as Coney Island, which catered to the newly ambitious recreational tastes of the urban masses.[7]

Many of these other expositions paid a candid tribute, in their promotional efforts and official publications, to the fair that was undeniably the most spectacular and most successful version of the genre. Occasionally others attempted to go beyond the Chicago event—in physical size St. Louis was bigger—and to claim additional distinctions. But the formative influence of the World's Columbian Exposition was undeniable.

And so was its inspirational role for urban institutions and urban plans. Although the City Beautiful movement had origins older than the fair, and powerful contemporary influences came from the achievements of European cities, the White City continued to be a major presence in American city life. Many architects, landscape planners, sculptors, and painters involved with the exposition would, over the next twenty years, devote themselves to hundreds of municipal improvement projects, decorated buildings, city parks, enhanced waterfronts, ennobled railroad stations, widened streets and boulevards, museum buildings, and libraries.[8] Likewise, fair promoters found themselves serving on the boards of museums of art and natural history, of zoos and orchestras, and of public improvement leagues and civic reform associations. Every time a great city plan was published—for Chicago or San Francisco or Cleveland or Denver—even by architects who were not directly involved with the Columbian Exposition, it was difficult to avoid some sense of resonance, even if indirect.[9] In some of these plans, memories of the exposition were invoked as selling points, suggestions that the utopian visions being offered were neither impossible nor unprecedented, given the grand landscape achieved in Jackson Park.

Individual structures—such as Union Station in Washington, D.C., Pennsylvania Station in New York City, or the new Field Museum in Chicago—recalled the outlines and sometimes the details of the exposition. Locally, the association was especially strong, for Daniel Burnham's 1909 Chicago plan was promoted, in the teens, by a decade-long crusade that drew on the fair's glories.[10]

Publications also may have contributed to lively immediate memories, although perhaps a bit less than might have been expected. Much of this literature was official—government reports, management statements, commemorative histories—and emerged with surprising speed. The fair's elaborate organization and multiple sources of revenue required painstaking narration. And the scale of the exposition fed a delight in quantification. An imposing mass of details—daily admissions figures and temperatures, concession attendance and sales, special days and events, building costs, payrolls, meetings held, speeches given, medals and certificates awarded, construction hours, freight received and shipped, food served, garbage disposed of, commercial participants, accidents, lawsuits, crime, transportation numbers—were tabulated, organized, listed, analyzed by the authorities, and placed within multivolume sets.[11] Exposition literature was dominated by these large and intimidating monuments to managerial self-consciousness and public accountability.

Such publications had long been produced for foreign expositions. Five-volume sets summarized the Americans' efforts in Paris in 1878 and 1889, placing the national contribution in juxtaposition to foreign presentations, using these fairs as moments to gauge points of national strength and

Souvenirs from the world's fair of 1893: right, Christopher Columbus badge; left and below, assorted admission tickets.

The Chicago world's fair of 1893 influenced the design of future international expositions. The Omaha Trans-Mississippi International Exposition of 1898, *opposite,* as well as the Buffalo Pan-American Exposition of 1901, *top left,* and the St. Louis Louisiana Purchase Exposition of 1904, *top right,* all reinforced the beaux-arts architectural plan of Chicago's fair. Even the Ferris Wheel, introduced at the World's Columbian Exposition, reappeared in the St. Louis fair in 1904, *bottom.*

weakness.[12] In Chicago, an American-run fair, there was no reason for such a report, but quite a few individual states—Utah, Kansas, Iowa, New York, and Connecticut among them—and a number of countries did publish special illustrated texts on their own buildings and displays.[13]

The documents appeared with surprising punctuality, most of the official reports, along with catalogues and interpretive materials, emerging in 1893 and 1894. Of the 316 Columbian Exposition publications listed in a Smithsonian Institution bibliography—guidebooks, reports, catalogues, statements, and circulars—only nine appeared after 1894. And some of these were partly issued before this date.[14] The latecomers included, to be sure, several quite significant pieces, among them the later volumes of the authoritative history of the exposition by Rossiter Johnson, and the report of the commissioner general. But, paradoxically enough, the release of the official documents came so close on the heels of the fair that they were not given much attention. It is difficult to find much reviewer response in contemporary magazines. The size and density of these publications, as well as a national consciousness that was sated with fair events, may have accounted for their failure to be noticed. For decades these bulky volumes lingered in secondhand bookstores or on little-used library shelves. Such neglect has obscured not only the care with which they were prepared, but also the expectation that the information they provided would be exploited by grateful audiences. To all but specialists, however, they were about as exciting as census reports. Later historians have found the tabulations, the classification systems, the photographic reproductions, and the entire system of assumptions to be fascinating revelations of the values inspiring expositions and the world view the fair projected.

In these initial years, however, public opinion may not have needed the stimulation of these reports to keep its sense of the fair fresh, given the many other contemporary events that did so. Thirty years later, with so many great events intervening, it was a different matter. The fair was now increasingly distant and exotic, a setting that children's books could

A silver pin, top, representing Columbus's caravel, the Santa Maria, and right, a Wedgwood plate decorated with a transfer of the Administration Building were among the souvenirs that appealed to popular taste.

employ to entrance their young readers, a never-never land.[15] City planning and a new phase of neo-classical architecture had implanted themselves so firmly on the landscape that they had begun to form their own tradition.

The fair's reputation itself had begun to suffer. By the end of the 1920s there was an increasing tendency to view it as both a stylistic embarrassment and, in planning terms, an unfortunate mistake, wildly popular though it may once have been. As part of a much larger shift of attitudes and sensibilities, modernism was being preached as an appropriate response to the new age of skyscrapers and automobiles, a modernism that for some architects meant reclaiming structural honesty and freeing design from subservience to historical references. While the decade continued to produce large numbers of highly traditional art objects, monuments, and buildings, the voices of rebel artists and critics gained credibility.[16]

In Chicago, the contest over the memory of the Columbian Exposition was particularly spirited. Local pride granted special attention to the writings and opinions of Louis Sullivan. Sullivan's attack on the fair—printed some thirty years after the event and several years after his own death—included the most quoted paragraphs and summed up the gist of the post–World War I repudiation. His critique appeared in the very last pages of his *Autobiography of an Idea*, written during the final and most bitter phase of an increasingly unhappy life and published in 1924. While the single most-cited sentence, "The damage wrought by the World's Fair will last for half a century from its date, if not longer," catches Sullivan's negative stance, it does not capture the extraordinary depth of his resentment nor

These colorfully printed paper fans enabled viewers to recall the White City. Top, bird's-eye perspective. Bottom, vignettes of the major buildings in the Court of Honor.

Souvenirs were available for purchase on the Midway. This unusual "theater," right, allowed the viewer to scroll images of the major buildings across the stage by turning wooden knobs. Glassware from the Libbey Pavilion, below, commemorating the world's fair could even be personalized. The ruby glass pitcher reads, "Nellie Baker from her husband July 18, 1893."

the pungent imagery he employed. In bursts of witty infuriation he referred to the Illinois Pavilion at the fair as a "lewd exhibit of drooling imbecility," while the larger inspiration for the fair, the "feudal idea," he labeled a "white cloud." Sullivan employed a series of biological metaphors to link enthusiasm for the fair with disease. The multitude of visitors to Chicago in 1893, he argued, had no time to become "immune" to this sophistication. They were departing as "carriers of contagion," subject to a "virus" that "contaminated" the rest of the country in a "violent outbreak" of the classical and the Renaissance, aided by "deep-seated illusions, hallucinations, absence of pupillary reaction to light, absence of knee-reaction—symptoms all of progressive cerebral meningitis: The blanketing of the brain. Thus Architecture died in the land of the free and the home of the brave."[17]

Sullivan's mordancy was more extreme than anyone else's. But the passion that underlay his assault appealed by its very sincerity, even to those who might have been expected to extend greater sympathy to the fair's memory. By this time the major principals—Richard Morris Hunt, Daniel Burnham, McKim, Mead & White—were long since dead, although some of their colleagues and many of their disciples had become the busiest architects in America. While artists such as Edwin Blashfield and Daniel Chester French remained alive, most of the muralists and sculptors—Augustus Saint-Gaudens, Kenyon Cox, Francis Millet—had also gone, their successors, in the immediate post–Armory Show era, struggling against the challenge of aggressive modernists who threatened, in the 1920s, to sweep faculty appointments, prize contests, and museum purchases away from the ranks of the orthodox.[18]

The Sullivan attack was especially memorable and influential, then, but it did not stand alone. Singling out the exposition as the source and symbol of reactionary power, repression, dishonesty, and grandiosity fit the iconoclastic mood of many critics in the 1920s. Henry-Russell Hitchcock labeled it the "white plague" and, citing the remark decades later, Thomas A. P. Van Leeuwen observes that the exposition was apparently regarded with "something akin to hatred."[19] In the work of critics and historians like Van Wyck Brooks, Vernon Louis Parrington, Thomas Beer, H. L. Mencken, a tone of bemused outrage at the presumption, pomposity, and hypocrisy of earlier generations was palpable. Sullivan's outraged tones were most closely echoed by one of the more learned and long-lived of these commentators, Lewis Mumford. His celebration of Sullivan, Frederick Law Olmsted, and John A. Roebling in Brown Decades, published in 1931, created new cultural heroes. But five years earlier he had submitted his major indictment of the Columbian Exposition in Sticks & Stones.

In a chapter entitled "The Imperial Facade," Mumford tendered the fair as an apt demonstration of America's new age, one in which industrial trust and political power were used as tools against popular interests. "The keys to this period are opulence and magnitude," he remarked. The fair consolidated the age's stylistic tendencies, imitating Rome because of "its stereotyped canons and rules—because of the relatively small number of choices it offered for a lapse in taste—because of its skill in conspicuous waste, and because of that very noncommittal quality in its massive forms which permitted the basilica to become a church, or the temple to become a modern bank."[20] Mumford

attacked the taste for veneer—the staff covering steel and glass structures. But the greatest evil of the fair, Mumford concluded, was its suggestion to "the civic enthusiast that every city might become a fair," applying the City Beautiful idea as "a sort of municipal cosmetic," a course that detoured around the more fundamental problems of urban congestion and mismanagement. Quoting Sullivan, Mumford deflected attacks on the fair's architects themselves, in favor of blaming larger social conditions. Inevitably, he insisted, such conditions were what shaped the fair's forms and ideals. "It would be foolish to reproach the great run of architects for exploiting the characteristics of their age," Mumford explained, because architecture, like government, "is about as good as a community deserves."[21] The world's fair, in short, exemplified a civilization that provided "grandiloquent stones for people who have been deprived of bread and sunlight and all that keeps man from becoming vile." The "monumental facades" of the city beautiful hid "a landless proletariat, doomed to the servile routine of the factory system," a "countryside whose goods are drained away . . . and whose remaining cultivators are steadily drifting into the ranks of an abject tenantry."[22]

Mumford's broadly argued attack on what he believed to be the corruption of American ideals was the most enveloping contemporary assault on the White City. Unlike some earlier dissenters, such as William Dean Howells who detected in the landscape of Jackson Park hints of better, more cooperative days to come and alternative symbols to the late nineteenth century's ferocious competitiveness, Mumford found the fair's order tyrannical and dangerous.

In Louis Sullivan's opinion contemporary enthusiasts of neoclassical imitations symbolized "the pallid academic mind, denying the real, exhalting the fictitious and the false, incapable of adjusting itself to the flow of living things, to the reality and the pathos of man's follies." Portrait by Frank A. Werner, 1919.

The Museum of Science and Industry now occupies the World's Columbian Exposition's Palace of Fine Arts, photographed here, top, in 1893 by C. D. Arnold.

Chicago's Century of Progress Exposition, held in 1933, looked to a future enhanced by scientific and technological advances. Right: Travel and Transportation Building. Facing page: The 1933 Skyride provided thrillseekers with a bird's-eye view of the fairgrounds as had the Ferris Wheel in the 1893 fair.

Few of Mumford's contemporaries had either the courage or the energy to honor all his charges, but many adapted them to their own needs. The fair, as a serious exercise in planning and idealism, became something of a bad joke to progressive designers. But Chicago's citizens remained bound by nostalgic attachment to its last remaining palace, today's Museum of Science and Industry, in ruins for much of the 1920s and 1930s. Many found their chief pleasure in recalling the Midway and the Ferris Wheel rather than the Court of Honor.

The fair's memory, moreover, was increasingly architectural and stylistic rather than social or cultural. The attacks, coupled with the increasing distance of time, transformed the fair into a metaphor. It provoked discussion, naturally enough, during the planning for Chicago's second great fair, the 1933 Century of Progress Exposition, but the later fair made few allusions to its predecessor. Its emphasis on science and technology rather than art, its self-consciously modernistic structures, and its location all contrasted rather than connected the two expositions. In his 1952 text, *Fair Management*, Lenox Lohr, manager of the Century of Progress, referred to the White City only occasionally, and often to differentiate it from the later exposition.[23] The "Aladdin City" of 1933 had about it "simplicity and usability rather than elegance," Paul Gilbert told prospective visitors. "No 'exposition art,' no gingerbread about Chicago's second World's Fair City. No suggestion of the glory that was Greece. Nothing you have ever seen before."[24] Acknowledging the "magnificent gesture" of the old White City, backers of this fair emphasized modernity and corporate progress. "A Century of Progress Exposition, it was determined, must be more than a historic pageant. It must depart from tradition and express creatively the spirit of the new age. It must tear away the veil that shrouds the future."[25]

Like the Century of Progress, the other fairs of the 1930s—New York and San Francisco hosted the most impressive versions—were modernistic and futuristic in their orientation, making little acknowledgment to the White City in either their planning or their rhetoric.[26] And the cumulative impact of the depression, the New Deal, and World War II did little to revitalize interest in the Columbian Exposition. If anything, the miseries of the recession and the war encouraged breaks with the past. So much in the physical fabric of urban life required reconstruction, so much of the city's infrastructure appeared exhausted and outdated, that historical referencing was neither pervasive nor profound in the 1940s and 1950s. No longer were the ideals of the Columbian Exposition worth extensive attack. They had been so far buried that they would have had to have been resurrected first. The fiftieth anniversary of the fair took place during World War II and, as might be expected, attracted little attention.

After the war, with the huge movement of people and investments to the suburbs, the urban situation grew much more desperate. Many metropolitan traditions seemed even less relevant with the explosion of tract houses and shopping centers that surrounded most American cities. Remnants of the city's architectural heritage—labeled cumbersome, grimy, and outdated—disappeared as bulldozers created the spaces for new commercial or industrial development. High-rise modernism set the tone. World's fairs, of whatever variety, were not in fashion. Historians paid respectful homage to the fairs as influences on national traditions of urban

KAUFMANN - FABRY

As memories of the World's Columbian Exposition faded, the city's strength continued to rest upon manufacturing and distribution. In this 1941 photograph railroads are bypassing beaux-arts classicism as they race north from Illinois Central Railroad yard. Photograph by Andreas Feininger.

Facing page: Demolition of the Federal Building and Post Office, 1965. "Worn-out" symbols of the past were bulldozed to make way for the "renewal" of the urban landscape.

planning, but they were, for the most part, treated as somewhat embarrassing stage sets, unconnected to the real futures of American urban areas, and something of a detour on the march to progress.

Historians of Chicago and of the period largely sustained the older charges of irrelevancy and falsity. Thus Ray Ginger, in *Altgeld's America*, repeated the earlier accusation that Burnham was a great executive rather than a great architect. The steel frames were coated with stucco-like staff, an "absurd" surfacing for Chicago, and "the idea was to copy, and to decorate in a way that had little or no relation to the structure . . . to the life of the city. Here was enormous energy but no vision." What people sought was "the sensational, the saccharine, the easily understood."[27] Seven years later, in a far more subtle presentation, Hugh Dalziel Duncan continued to embroider upon the Sullivan picture, developing another old theme, that John Root, had he lived, would have developed a far different, more colorful and fiery fair. The title of one chapter caught Duncan's argument succinctly: "The Defeat of the Chicago School at the World's Fair, Chicago Yields to the East."[28]

But then, even while scholars and chroniclers were sustaining the older attitudes, starting in the sixties a series of trends developed that would give American world's fairs, and the Columbian Exposition in particular, a renewed hold on public interest. The trends were anticipated to some extent, in earlier decades. But the pace and intensity were new.

This decade, in spite of its radical assaults on conventional behavior and tradition, served as the breeding ground for the nostalgia constituency—collectors, dealers, journalists, curators, historians, and advertising specialists—committed to

recovering and publicizing the physical remnants of the American past. In particular, there emerged a new emphasis on popular, mass-produced items, frequently associated with commercial distributors. Soon flea markets, clubs, specialized museums, societies, newsletters, price lists, directories, encyclopedias, and catalogues appeared. By the 1970s desire had swelled into a passion. In 1978 Time-Life Books published a sixteen-volume *Encyclopedia of Collectibles*, with almost two hundred categories, ranging from advertising giveaways and baseball cards to playing cards and toasters. World's fairs, of course, were well represented. A number of Americans had begun to rediscover the immense mass of objects that were originally designed to keep the fair fresh in the popular imagination—its souvenirs.

What caused this preoccupation? Many things can be adduced: inflation and a renewed respect for the appreciating value of old objects; increased leisure; a new generation of hobbyists; more populist attitudes toward history and historical change; the influence of electronic mass media; preservation consciousness; curiosity; easier modes of travel and communication. But whatever the fundamental causes, world's fairs, as major purveyors of nostalgia, benefited considerably as subjects of speculation, and the most formidable among them was the World's Columbian Exposition.

The creation of a World's Fair Collectors Society demonstrated the centrality of fairs to the developing nostalgia. If many were drawn to souvenirs, commercial antiques, and paper ephemera because they found the past more charming, more exciting, and more picturesque, the fairs were natural stopping points. In essence, with their concentrated dis-

plays of object-filled landscapes, fairs summed up older values. Their self-confident rhetoric may have seemed reassuring to atomic age pessimists. The range of activities, the lavish arrays of art and technology, and the innovative entertainments all served to make the expositions' appeal irresistible.

And so did their locations in great cities. If in the 1940s and 1950s triumphant modernism branded older expositions as irrelevant, the 1960s, and even more, the 1970s and 1980s, suggested something heroic about the ambitious landscape plans the fairs exemplified, particularly when juxtaposed with the maddeningly slow pace and obstacle-strewn path of current urban renewal programs. Austerely decorated facades, glass towers, huge apartment complexes, invasive road systems, immense garages, littered and inadequate park systems, billboarded avenues, and abandoned waterfronts all contrasted with the monumental, symmetrical, sparkling, highly decorated settings that had been the expositions' legacy. The authoritarianism and historicist conceits that had so angered Louis Sullivan and his colleagues no longer seemed as important to newer urban reformers, whose revulsion from modernism was demonstrated also by their attachment to the growing preservation movement. As old office buildings, city halls, apartment houses, and commercial complexes fell victim to the wrecking ball, protests mounted against destruction of an architectural heritage.[29] Again, fairs like the Columbian Exposition, although they had been constructed in part to renovate and correct the chaos of their own landscapes, seemed to symbolize more humane values, and to suggest, paradoxically, the greater efficiency of the nineteenth- and early twentieth-century planners when it came to creating urban infrastructures and great public works.

Thus scholarly writing about the White City, when it began to reappear in the 1960s and 1970s, reflected a growing sense of interest in its urban planning philosophy and in the achievement of Daniel Burnham, chief of construction. It had taken until the 1970s for Burnham to receive his first modern biography and for McKim, Mead and White to gain credible reexamination, a reflection of the long night of neglect that beaux-arts designs had undergone and of the lack of interest in the orthodox traditions of pre-modern American architecture.[30]

But the new enthusiasm was genuine.[31] It is unfortunate, wrote one architect introducing a reprinting of Burnham's *Plan of Chicago* in 1970, that "Sullivan's later writings painted a picture" of the Columbian Exposition "not entirely consistent with what modern scholars are just beginning to recognize as a triumph of early modern planning if not of architecture."[32] The White City, wrote another scholar a few years later, "demonstrated the order and beauty that advance planning makes possible"; its advances in technology, traffic, and sanitation "gave people experience and faith—faith that a new kind of urban life could become a reality."[33] Exhibitions on Burnham, City Beautiful planning, public murals, other expositions, and fair photography further solidified the new respect for the vision and skill of those who were in charge of the exposition.[34] By comparison, late twentieth-century planners and designers seemed weak and confused.

Intellectual and cultural historians of the 1970s and early 1980s were also attracted to the Columbian Exposition for some of the very reasons that repelled Sullivan and some of the post–World War I

The World's Columbian Exposition of 1893 celebrated the four-hundredth anniversary of Christopher Columbus's voyage. The fair was delayed one year due to organizational delays. Facing page: Small metal statuette of Columbus. Top: Isabella bracelet with love tokens. Left and below: Medals awarded at the fair for exemplary products.

critics: its sweeping synthetic effort to create symbols of solidarity for a civilization that often seemed fragmented and divided.[35] Marching across North America, absorbing millions of immigrants, and playing with ideas of a new people "happily endowed with the best attributes of all the world's races," Americans were "looking for a sign. Suddenly in the heart of the continent that sign appeared," wrote David Huntington, one of the new school of appreciative historians. Chicago's "imperial dream" blended "into one whole, the guises of Athens and Rome, Florence and Venice, Paris and Versailles" that "made America's collective vision a reality—for one wonderful moment."[36]

Admitting that the fair's vision was "contrived," and that its artistic and architectural styles formed "an insult to native American genius," another recent historian nevertheless found it to be "a positive response" to the prevailing psychological needs of the day. "In the White City," wrote Reid Badger, "Chicago and the country at large got what they felt they needed to counterbalance the materialism they feared, the confusion of traditional values and symbols, the lack of cultural and political leadership, and the dislocations they were experiencing." It was indeed an illusion, but "as an illusion it did not have to conform to the everyday practical realities of American life," as Sullivan wished.[37]

And, in 1979, in an influential catalogue accompanying the Brooklyn Museum's American Renaissance show, Richard Guy Wilson questioned a historiography that had for decades "either ignored or deplored" the American Renaissance and pointed out that "the most enjoyable and comprehensible elements of cities" were frequently those parts inspired by their values and practices.[38] The catalogue reveled in photographs and drawings from the exposition, and work from its participating artists and architects such as McKim, Mead and White, Augustus Saint-Gaudens, Edwin H. Blashfield, and Daniel Chester French.

Finally, in the 1970s, a growing revolt against the tenets of orthodox modernism, a surge of critiques and dissatisfactions that had many sources and took many forms, provided a forum for both preachers of eclecticism and for postmodernist apostles of decoration and adornment. If the exposition palaces were little more than "decorated sheds," as some architectural historians had earlier described them, the decorated shed as a building type had assumed new significance in the world that was learning to learn from Las Vegas, and from Robert Venturi, Denise Scott Brown, Charles Moore, Robert A. M. Stern, and other designers. In both its neoclassical and its commercial phases, it seemed, the fair was an anticipation of things to come.

These trends, excitement about the possibilities of fairs in general and the Columbian Exposition in particular, climaxed in Chicago during the early and mid-eighties, when Mayor Jane Byrne spearheaded a drive to create a new exposition in 1992. Extensive lobbying brought approval from the Paris-based Bureau of International Expositions. A site, revised and amended several times, was chosen, and architects gathered to draw up initial plans. But the challenges of unifying competing constituencies, solving environmental problems, and, above all, avoiding damage to the vulnerable credit of the state of Illinois (which was being asked to honor the revenue bonds that would be issued) were too much.[39] They combined to defeat an enterprise that sought,

The architectural legacy of the World's Columbian Exposition is evident in both Burnham and Company's plan for Union Station (facing page) and Daniel Burnham and Edward Bennett's 1909 Plan of Chicago (above). The City Beautiful movement, strengthened by memories of the Court of Honor, influenced civic planning in many American cities.

self-consciously, at moment of diminished expectations, to revive Chicago's glory.

These quadruple routes to a more active and affirmative acknowledgement of the exposition—tributes to nostalgia, urban planning, symbolic unity, and new stylistic relevance—however qualified and hedged they were by concessions to contemporary criticism, would soon be countered by a far darker vision that echoed, with a different vocabulary, the spirit of Sullivan's antihegemonic critique of a half-century earlier. The principal target, however, was no longer architecture. It was the value system projected by the exposition, which in turn was the value system of the cultural, economic, and political establishments of the day.[40] Treating the world's fairs seriously now required examinations that went beyond details of their physical plants or dominant building styles. The expositions, with their concentrated cultural messages, appeared to some scholars as instruments in the hands of dominant social interests. Behind the public enthusiasm and popular approval of the fairgrounds and the midways lay campaigns of propaganda and promotion with highly specific objectives. Historians were finding cultural politics in a variety of venues—commercial advertising, retail stores, museums, tourism, pageants, theme parks, parades, public rituals, educational and philanthropic institutions. To these were added the world's fairs and, most notably, the White City as an exemplary demonstration of social mastery.[41]

Thus Alan Trachtenberg made the Columbian Exposition his final chapter in a text examining America's Gilded Age. The White City appeared to have settled the "true and real meaning of America," enthroning elite culture and marginalizing the

*Drawings of the proposed
1992 Chicago world's fair,
which never took place.*

This illustration from History of the World's Columbian Exposition *(1893)* envisions idealized women as symbols of creativity.

"low." "It seemed the victory of elites in business, politics, and culture over dissident but divided voices of laborers, farmers, immigrants, blacks and women. . . . It [was] a culmination of the efforts of ruling groups since the Civil War to win hegemony over the emerging national culture," and "a prophetic symbol of the coming defeat of Populism and its alternative culture, the alternative 'America' it proposed."[42]

Trachtenberg argued that the exposition's master plan, its organization of spaces, its system of adornment, and its method of composition constituted an incorporation of "contrary and diverse values" to support a single system of culture and social values.[43] M. Christine Boyer wrote about the same time that, in the wake of the White City, the American urban ideal "posited eternal order and civic meaning in place of physical disorder, personal void, and political and economic exploitation." Neglecting the actual motives and energies of contemporary city life, "the neoclassical mode offered only a formalized view. How, then, could the public gaze perceive a moral and civic message from among such alienated displays of order and purity?"[44] Peter Hales, examining the photography of the fair, argued that the exposition "represented the peak of a consolidating movement, whereby an American urban elite gained control over the production of the urban vision."[45]

In keeping with a range of newly expressed concerns, a number of students of the exposition reexamined the role played by women and the exclusionary policies that constrained black participation in the fair. The protests expressed by black leaders at the time were vigorous and elo-

quent; they were also, as historians have shown, on the whole unsuccessful in their struggle against contemporary bigotry.[46] The story of women at the fair has been more complex and contested.[47] As the debate over the meaning and impact of "separate spheres" for men and women has grown, so the strategies deployed at the exposition to present female achievements have been subjected to increasingly critical scrutiny.

Other scholars have drawn out of an apparent miscellany of private concessions, public exhibits, and corporate displays a coherent if reactionary set of messages.[48] These themes positioned and characterized groups of people, activities and professions, areas of the world, and "scientific" principles. The White City and the Midway were "two sides of the same coin—a coin minted in the tradition of American racism, in which the forbidden desires of whites were projected onto dark-skinned peoples, who consequently had to be degraded so white purity could be maintained," wrote Robert W. Rydell in his influential study of American expositions.[49] The fairs of the era between the 1870s and World War I were "triumphs of hegemony as well as symbolic edifices," the "exercise of economic and political power in cultural terms by the established leaders of American society."[50] In speaking of expositions as informal educations, the promoters of the 1893 fair were more accurate than they imagined, as well as less benevolent than they assumed.

Holders of very different itineraries have thus been lured to the Columbian Exposition. Nostalgic accumulation, pietistic evocation, textual decoding, and ideological assault have little in common beyond their concern with fairs as physical enterprises. But then many fair visitors and commentators of the 1890s had varying agendas as well. What we now must acknowledge is the richness of these international expositions, not merely as putative symbols of unity, trophies of class victory, or emblems of triumphant progress, but as unique records of sometimes hidden contest and often disguised confrontation. Governed by rules that today often seem inequitable or outdated, the fairs, in the very acts of codifying and formulating, constituted statements of value and priority. The White City stands today not as a dream-like vision. Instead it has become the embodiment of a vanished world, more quickly responsive to our questions about nineteenth-century America than is the society that lay around it. In one of history's characteristic reversals, that temporary, evanescent, and fragile wisp of an event, six months old at its death, has outlasted the solidly permanent forces and institutions that gave it birth. Our current commemorations of the fair can celebrate, at least, this victory over time and decay.

This Javanese woman, interrupted from her self-examination in a mirror, returns an enigmatic gaze to the viewer.

NOTES

1. The Field Columbian Museum was housed in the Fine Arts Palace and remained there until a new building for the Field was completed after World War I; the Fine Arts Palace would later be renovated by Julius Rosenwald for today's Museum of Science and Industry. Other buildings that stood for some years included the German Building and a Japanese Tea House on the Wooded Island.

2. The controversies over photography at the exposition are described in Peter B. Hales, *Silver Cities: The Photography of American Urbanization, 1839–1915* (Philadelphia: Temple University Press, 1984), 131–59.

3. See Paul Connerton, *How Societies Remember* (Cambridge: Cambridge University Press, 1989), 5, for one definition. For Coser's remark see Maurice Halbwachs, *On Collective Memory*, Lewis A. Coser, ed. and trans., (Chicago: University of Chicago Press, 1992), 34.

4. The fair's total attendance was recorded as something over 25 million. This figure probably contains some padding, and it certainly included many repeat visitors. Just how many is unclear, but an estimate of somewhere between 12 and 16 million seems reasonable.

5. For the range of souvenirs produced by the fair see Howard M. Rossen and John M. Kaduck, *Columbian World's Fair Collectibles Chicago (1892–1893): A Collector's Descriptive Price Guide* (Des Moines, IA: Wallace Homestead Book Co., 1976).

6. The most recent comprehensive treatment of these expositions and their relationship to the White City can be found in Robert W. Rydell, *All the World's a Fair: Visions of Empire at American International Expositions, 1876–1916* (Chicago: University of Chicago Press, 1984).

7. Some of the concessions are treated in John F. Kasson, *Amusing the Millions* (New York: Hill and Wang, 1978), 50–54.

8. The most recent comprehensive treatment of this era of city planning is William H. Wilson, *The City Beautiful Movement* (Baltimore: Johns Hopkins University Press, 1989).

9. This was particularly true of the plan for Washington, D.C., which involved Daniel Burnham. John W. Reps, in his history of urban planning, joined the exposition with the Washington plan in his final chapter. See John W. Reps, *The Making of Urban America: A History of City Planning in the United States* (Princeton: Princeton University Press, 1965), chap. 18.

10. For the campaign see Thomas J. Schlereth, "Burnham's Plan and Moody's Manual: City Planning as Progressive Reform," *Journal of the American Planning Association* 47 (Jan. 1981), 70–82, reprinted in Thomas J. Schlereth, *Cultural History and Material Culture: Everyday Life, Landscapes, Museums* (Ann Arbor, MI: UMI Research Press, 1990), 235–62.

11. The most elaborate of these was Rossiter Johnson, ed., *A History of the World's Columbian Exposition Held in Chicago in 1893*, 4 vols. (New York: D. Appleton and Company, 1897).

12. *Reports of the United States Commissioners to the Paris Universal Exposition, 1878*, 5 vols. (Washington, D.C.: Government Printing Office, 1880); *Reports of the United States Commissioners to the Universal Exposition of 1889 at Paris*, 5 vols. (Washington, D.C.: Government Printing Office, 1890–91).

13. Among them were California, Iowa, Kansas, New York, Pennsylvania, and, of course, Illinois.

14. See *The Books of the Fairs: Materials about World's Fairs, 1834–1915, in the Smithsonian Institution Libraries* (Chicago: American Library Association, 1992), 146–74. For more on the World's Columbian Exposition, see the recently published G. L. Dybwad, *Annotated Bibliography: World's Columbian Exposition, Chicago, 1893* (Albuquerque, NM: Book Stops Here, 1992).

15. For example, George R. Sparks, *The Dream City: A Story of the World's Fair* (Chicago: W. B. Conkey Company, 1923). Doris, Bobbie, and Joan enjoy themselves one summer in Jackson Park, talking about the wonders of 1893.

16. The story of stylistic debate in this decade is quite complex. For one detailed analysis of how classicism and modernism confronted one another in a single city, along with the tensions among competing versions of classicism and attempts to define legitimate lines of architectural descent, see David B. Brownlee, *Building the City Beautiful: The Benjamin Franklin Parkway and the Philadelphia Museum of Art* (Philadelphia: Philadelphia Museum of Art, 1989).

17. Louis H. Sullivan, *The Autobiography of an Idea* (New York: Press of the American Institute of Architects, 1924), 318–26.

18. For more on these debates and the embattled traditionalists see George H. Roeder, Jr., *Forum of Uncertainty: Confrontations with Modern Painting in Twentieth-Century American Thought* (Ann Arbor, MI: UMI Research Press, 1980).

19. Thomas A. P. van Leeuwen, *The Skyward Trend of Thought: Five Essays on the Metaphysics of the American Skyscraper* (The Hague: AHA Books, 1986), 21.

20. Lewis Mumford, *Sticks & Stones: A Study of American Architecture and Civilization* (New York: Boni and Liveright, 1924), 125, 128.

21. Ibid., 150.

22. Ibid., 148.

23. Lenox R. Lohr, *Fair Management: The Story of A Century of Progress Exposition: A Guide for Future Fairs* (Chicago: Cuneo Press, 1952), 8, 36, 101, 192, 200. These references to the 1893 fair, while brief, were often admiring.

24. Paul T. Gilbert, "A Century of Progress Exposition, Herald of a New Age: Interpreting Creatively the Spirit of Today" in Glenn A. Bishop, comp., *Chicago's Accomplishments and Leaders* (Chicago: Bishop Publishing, 1932), 146. Gilbert allowed that the 1893 fair was a "magnificent gesture," making Chicago the Queen City of the world. "No exposition held since that time has been able to compare with it either in its ineffable, dream-like beauty or in the splendor of its exhibits. It ushered in a renaissance of classic[al] architecture." Ibid., 146.

25. Ibid., 150.

26. See John G. Cawelti, "America on Display, 1876–1893, 1933," in Frederic C. Jaher, ed., *The Age of Industrialism in America* (New York: Free Press, 1968), 317–63.

27. Ray Ginger, *Altgeld's America: The Lincoln Ideal Versus Changing Realities* (New York: Funk & Wagnalls, 1958), 18, 21.

28. Hugh Dalziel Duncan, *Culture and Democracy: The Struggle for Form in Society and Architecture in Chicago and the Middle West during the Life and Times of Louis H. Sullivan* (Totowa, NJ: Bedminster Press, 1965), chaps. 37–39. Duncan reviewed the historiography of the fair, tracing the different emphases of Charles Moore (city planner and biographer of Burnham), Harriet Monroe, and the architectural historian, Thomas E. Tallmadge.

29. "By all indices—public and private support, membership growth in professional organizations, innovative new programs—the decade between the passage of the National Historic Preservation Act in 1966 and the Bicentennial Year of 1976 was the most significant the American preservation movement has experienced." *Where to Look: A Guide to Preservation Information* (Washington, D.C.: Advisory Council on Historic Preservation, 1982), 2. The major history of American historic preservation, Charles B. Hosmer, Jr., *Preservation Comes of Age: From Williamsburg to the National Trust, 1926–1949*, 2 vols. (Charlottesville, VA: University of Virginia Press, 1981), ends just before this tremendous period of growth, and the story of the next four decades has yet to be fully documented. Hosmer's afterword is suggestive about this period, and a series of texts have appeared on adaptive reuse, tax strategies for preservation, gentrification, and similar matters. For events leading up to and just following passage of the Historic Preservation Act see James A. Glass, *The Beginnings of a New National Historic Preservation Program, 1957–1969* (Nashville, TN: American Association for State and Local History, 1990). Further suggestions can be found in James Marson Fitch, *Historic Preservation: Curatorial Management of the Built World* (New York: McGraw-Hill, 1982); Elizabeth Mulloy, *History of the National Trust for Historic Preservation* (Washington, D.C.: Preservation Press, 1976). In the mid-1970s a series of volumes explored lost buildings, notably Constance M. Greiff, ed., *Lost America: From the Atlantic to the Mississippi* (Princeton: Pyne Press, 1971); Nathan Silver, *Lost New York* (Boston: Houghton Mifflin, 1967); David Lowe, *Lost Chicago* (Boston: Houghton Mifflin, 1975); James M. Good, *Capital Losses: A Cultural History of Washington's Destroyed Buildings* (Washington, D.C.: Smithsonian Institution Press, 1979); Tony P. Wrenn and Elizabeth Mulloy, *America's Forgotten Architecture* (New York: Pantheon Books, 1976), while a host of illustrated books were devoted to documenting the past of the built environment, a taste that is still with us.

30. The Burnham biography was Thomas S. Hines, *Burnham of Chicago, Architect and Planner* (New York: Oxford University Press, 1974). This was the first book-length study of Burnham to appear for more than fifty years, since the appearance of Charles Moore, *Daniel H. Burnham: Architect, Planner of Cities*, 2 vols. (Boston: Houghton Mifflin, 1921). Interest in the firm of McKim, Mead and White was evidenced by a series of publications: Leland M. Roth, *McKim, Mead & White, Architects* (New York: Harper & Row, 1983); Richard Guy Wilson, *McKim, Mead & White, Architects* (New York: Rizzoli, 1983); Paul R. Baker, *Stanny: The Gilded Life of Stanford White* (New York: Free Press; London: Collier, Macmillan, 1989); and by a reprinting of an early twentieth-century work, *A Monograph of the Works of McKim, Mead & White, 1879–1915* (New York: Da Capo, 1985; orig. publ. 4 vols. 1915–1920). Other influential architects of the period attracting renewed attention included Richard Morris Hunt and Bertram Grosvenor Goodhue. See Paul R. Baker, *Richard Morris Hunt* (Cambridge, MA: MIT Press, 1980); Susan R. Stein, ed., *The Architecture of Richard Morris Hunt* (Chicago: University of Chicago Press, 1986); Richard Oliver, *Bertram Grosvenor Goodhue* (New York: Architectural History Foundation, 1983). For a broadly sympathetic but analytical treatment of the architecture of this era that reflects some of the revived interest, see Robert A. M. Stern, *Gregory Gilmartin, and John Massengale, New York 1900: Metropolitan Architecture and Urbanism, 1890–1915* (New York: Rizzoli, 1983); and for Chicago, and again a friendlier reexamination of European and beaux-arts influences, there is John Zukowsky, ed., *Chicago Architecture, 1872–1972: Birth of a Metropolis* (Chicago and Munich: Art Institute of Chicago and Prestel, 1988).

31. One might note also during this period the revived interest in beaux-arts architecture in France as well as the United States. See, among others, Arthur Drexler, ed., *The Architecture of the Ecole des Beaux-Arts* (New York: Museum of Modern Art, 1977); and Robin Middleton, ed., *The Beaux-Arts and Nineteenth-Century French Architecture* (Cambridge, MA.: MIT Press, 1982).

32. This was Wilbert R. Hasbrouck in his introduction to the reprinting of Daniel H. Burnham and Edward H. Bennett, *Plan of Chicago*, (New York: Da Capo, 1970), vi. The latest reprint is *Plan of Chicago* (New York: Princeton Architectural Press, 1992).

33. Sally Chappell, "Chicago Issues: The Enduring Power of a Plan," in *The Plan of Chicago: 1909–1979*, ed. John Zukowsky (Chicago: Art Institute of Chicago, 1979), 6. This exhibition honored the 70th anniversary of the plan, at a time of increasing interest in beaux-arts architectural traditions. It is also interesting to note the publication, in 1980, of one of the most helpful modern pictorial anthologies of the fair, Stanley Appelbaum, *The Chicago World's Fair of 1893: A Photographic Record* (New York: Dover, 1980). The author noted, just after his acknowledgments, the almost simultaneous appearance of the Brooklyn Museum exhibition, *The American Renaissance, 1876–1917*, and the publication of R. Reid Badger's *The Great American Fair: The World's Columbian Exposition and American Culture* (Chicago: Nelson-Hall, 1979).

34. Among others see the following texts and exhibition catalogues, published in the 1970s and 1980s, representing many parts of the country: *Temple of Justice: The Appellate Division Courthouse* (New York: House of the Association, 1977); Judd Kahn, *Imperial San Francisco: Politics and Planning in an American City, 1897–1906* (Lincoln, NE: University of Nebraska Press, 1979); *Jules Guerin: Master Delineator* (Houston, TX: Rice School of Architecture, 1983); *Past Futures: Two Centuries of Imagining Boston* (Cambridge, MA: Harvard Graduate School of Design, 1985); Carl Abbott, *The Great Extravaganza: Portland and the Lewis and Clark Exposition* (Portland: Oregon Historical Society, 1981); *The Great World's Fairs and Expositions* (Miami, FL: Mitchell Wolfson Jr. Collection of Decorative and Propaganda Arts, 1986); Carol McMichael, *Paul Cret at Texas: Architectural Drawing and the Image of the University in the 1930s* (Austin, TX: Archer M. Huntington Art Gallery, University of Texas, 1983); *Caltech 1910–1950: An Urban Architecture for Southern California* (Pasadena: Baxter Art Gallery, California Institute of Technology, 1983); Holly M. Rarick, *Progressive Vision: The Planning of Downtown Cleveland, 1903–1930* (Cleveland, OH: Cleveland Museum of Art and Indiana University Press, 1986); Joan E. Draper, *Edward H. Bennett: Architect and City Planner, 1874–1954* (Chicago: Art Institute of Chicago, 1982).

35. Not all of them, of course, reflected the new position. The Sullivan view remained popular among some. See, for example, Miles Orvell, *The Real Thing: Imitation and Authenticity in American Culture, 1880–1940* (Chapel Hill: University of North Carolina Press, 1989), 59–61.

36. David C. Huntington, essay titled *The Quest for Unity: American Art between World's Fairs, 1876–1893* (Detroit: Detroit Institute of Arts, 1983), 25. This, along with the Brooklyn Museum's *American Renaissance* exhibition of 1979, was one of the major museum presentations of the new sensibility.

37. Badger, *The Great American Fair*, 127.

38. Richard Guy Wilson, "The Great Tradition," in Richard Guy Wilson, Diane H. Pilgrim, and Richard R. Murray, *The American Renaissance 1876–1917* (Brooklyn: Brooklyn Museum and Pantheon, 1979), 70.

39. For an intelligent summary of the forces that helped defeat the 1992 proposal see Robert Hutchins, "The Planning of

the 1992 Chicago World's Fair," *Central: Papers on Architecture* (Winter 1987), 75–92.

40.   This must be viewed against a much larger historiographical background, a series of articles and texts subjecting institutional history, and cultural history more generally, to more critical examination and suggesting new boundaries to region, class, gender, and ethnicity. Within this larger literature, some references especially relevant to late nineteenth-century American culture should include T. J. Jackson Lears, *No Place of Grace: Anti-Modernism and the Transformation of American Culture* (New York: Pantheon, 1980); Francis G. Couvares, *The Remaking of Pittsburgh: Class and Culture in an Industrializing City, 1877–1919* (Albany: State University of New York Press, 1984); Lawrence W. Levine, *Highbrow/Lowbrow: The Emergence of Cultural Hierarchy in America* (Cambridge, MA.: Harvard University Press, 1988).

41.   And also of the struggles among commercial markets, play cultures, and ideal standards. See, among others, John F. Kasson, *Amusing the Millions: Coney Island at the Turn of the Century* (New York: Hill and Wang, 1978); and James Gilbert, *Perfect Cities: Chicago's Utopias of 1893* (Chicago: University of Chicago Press, 1991).

42.   Alan Trachtenberg, *The Incorporation of America: Culture and Society in the Gilded Age* (New York: Hill and Wang, 1982), 231.

43.   Ibid., 216.

44.   M. Christine Boyer, *Dreaming the Rational City: The Myth of American City Planning* (Cambridge, MA: The MIT Press, 1983), 50–51.

45.   Peter B. Hales, "Photography and the World's Columbian Exposition: A Case Study," *Journal of Urban History*, 15 (May 1989), 269. For another presentation of the Columbian Exposition as an expression of the values of Anglo-Saxon businessmen see Ellen M. Litwicki, "'The Inauguration of the People's Age': The Columbian Quadricentennial and American Culture," *Maryland Historian*, 20 (Spring/Summer 1987), 47–58.

46.   Both Frederick Douglass and Ida Wells wrote forcefully about the exclusion. See *The Reason Why the Colored American Is Not in the World's Columbian Exposition* (no imprint, 1893). In the 1960s and 1970s the episode was more closely examined. See Alfreda M. Duster, ed., *Crusade for Justice: The Autobiography of Ida B. Wells* (Chicago: University of

Chicago Press, 1970); Elliot M. Rudwick and August Meier, "Black Man in the 'White City': Negroes and the Columbia Exposition, 1893," *Phylon*, 26 (1965), 354–61; and Ann Massa, "Black Women in the 'White City,'" *Journal of American Studies*, 8 (Dec. 1974), 319–37.

47.   The modern historiography begins with the massive Jeanne Madeline Weimann, *The Fair Women: The Story of the Woman's Building, World's Columbian Exposition, Chicago 1893* (Chicago: Academy Chicago, 1981). It has been followed by other studies on figures such as Bertha Palmer, Sara Hallowell, Mary Cassatt, and Sophia Hayden, analyzing in more detail the struggle over representation.

48.   These analyses draw extensively upon the seminal work of European historians and theorists such as Michel Foucault and Antonin Gramsci, and on the implications of creating a society of spectacle. The museum and the international exposition are linked, as the crowd itself is transformed into a subject of observation and inspection. For one recent, broadly conceived such essay, see Tony Bennett, "The Exhibitionary Complex," *New Formations*, 4 (Spring 1988), 73–102.

49.   Robert W. Rydell, *All the World's a Fair: Visions of Empire at American International Expositions, 1876–1916* (Chicago: University of Chicago Press, 1984), 67. See also Rydell, "The World's Columbian Exposition of 1893: Racist Underpinnings of a Utopian Artifact," *Journal of American Culture*, 1 (Summer 1978), 253–75; and Raymond D. Fogelson, "The Red Man in the White City," in *Columbian Consequences*, David Hurst Thomas, ed. (Washington, D.C.: Smithsonian Institution Press, 1991), vol. 3, 73–90; Ira Jacknis, "Northwest Coast Indian Culture and the World's Columbian Exposition," in *Columbian Consequences*, Thomas, ed., vol. 3, 91–118; and Curtis M. Hinsley, "The World as Market Place: Commodification of the Exotic at the World's Columbian Exposition, Chicago, 1893," in Ivan Karp and Steven D. Lavine, eds., *Exhibiting Cultures: The Poetics and Politics of Museum Display* (Washington, D.C.: Smithsonian Institution Press, 1991), 344–65.

50.   Rydell, *All the World's a Fair*, 2.

The World's Columbian
Exposition of 1893,
*painting by Lawrence
Carmichael Earle.*

The Afterglow in the Lagoon, World's Columbian
Exposition, 1893, *Charles Caryl Coleman, oil on
wood panel, 1893.*

Opposite: Sunset Hour on the West Lagoon,
Willard L. Metcalf, oil on canvas.

U.S. Government Building, World's Columbian
Exposition, *painting by Childe Hassam.*

Mines and Mining Building, World's Columbian
Exposition, 1893, *Childe Hassam, watercolor on
cardboard*, 1893.

Administration Building, World's
Columbian Exposition, *painting by*
Charles Graham.

The Electricity Building, World's Columbian Exposition, *Charles Graham, watercolor on cardboard,* 1893.

The Golden Doorway of the Transportation Building,
Frank Russell Green, oil on canvas, 1893.

BUILDING AN ILLUSION

BUILDING AN ILLUSION: THE DESIGN OF THE WORLD'S COLUMBIAN EXPOSITION

by Wim de Wit

"Fighting the fair seems to be a favorite diversion. The pathway of the Columbian exposition is strewn with mementos of conflict."
Chicago Evening Post, *February 10, 1891*

In well-known images of the World's Columbian Exposition, such as C. D. Arnold's photographs of the grand exposition halls that lined the Court of Honor, the buildings appear to relate to one another with considerable ease. All are white, composed with similar arches and columns, and decorated with classically inspired sculpture. The buildings look as if they were created by a single designer, someone working independently and therefore capable of creating a total vision, a series of individual buildings that together make a strikingly unified statement.

Like its architecture, the 1893 World's Columbian Exposition itself may also seem, initially, as if it had been a unified, harmonious effort directed toward celebrating both the four-hundredth anniversary of Columbus's voyage to America and the progress made by the United States since that historic event. The many books published during and after 1893 to document the fair were emphatically promotional, suggesting that the intentions of the world's fair had been established without any disagreement.

The overall character of the World's Columbian Exposition emerged out of attitudes of cultural inferiority with which Americans in general, and Chicagoans in particular, were struggling during the last quarter of the nineteenth century. Chicagoans felt that they did not receive the recognition their city deserved from the urban centers on the East Coast, while Americans reacted to what they perceived as a lack of respect from Europe. Both groups believed others saw them as lacking in culture and, especially, as too young and inexperienced to be taken seriously. The design of the World's Columbian Exposition was directly affected by these perceptions of inferiority and the struggles for recognition they engendered. Comments by the fair organizers and architects reveal that the design of the fair was the result of a concerted effort to prove that the United States of America constituted a unified nation with a fully developed civilization of its own.

In the last quarter of the nineteenth century, many Americans felt a growing need to establish their nation as a leading power in the world. For the first time, the United States sought to expand its markets beyond the boundaries of its own continent.[1] As historian Frederick Jackson Turner announced to the

Architects Daniel Burnham and John Root, and landscape architects Frederick Law Olmsted and Henry Codman designed the layout of the fairgrounds.

World's Congress of Historians, one of a series of meetings held during the World's Columbian Exposition, the United States had become a country without any remaining frontiers.[2] Settlers had gone as far as the West Coast to develop new land and new markets, and the Pacific Ocean now prevented them from going any further. To continue to grow, East Coast industries needed to reach beyond their own continent, competing with foreign products and foreign countries. By the 1890s, as one historian has observed, "Expansion captivated the public as a whole as an expression of national power and vitality. Having at last established a unified nation, the people, albeit half-consciously, responded to appeals of 'pride,' 'duty,' and 'destiny' which seemed to confirm that success."[3]

Americans yearned for recognition of their unified nationhood from Europeans. Only then would Americans overcome the deep-seated feeling that, although their country was officially unified, it remained socially and culturally fragmented. In the nineteenth century, there was no better means of proving to the world that the United States was a real nation—a nation with a people united under one government and with a cultural tradition of its own—than a world's fair. Not only would a fair enable the United States to showcase its products and place them in competition with products of other countries, but it also allowed this country to compete on a cultural level with France, the nation identified with high culture. Paris had hosted a highly successful fair in 1889, just as Americans were beginning to think about a fair of their own.

Hosting a world's fair represented a valuable opportunity for Chicago as well. Less than sixty years old in 1890 and boasting one million inhabi-

tants, Chicago had grown with the Midwest by producing the tools that allowed farmers to cultivate large tracts of land and by providing facilities in which cattle from all over the region could be slaughtered. The entire center of the city (and large stretches to the north and south) had burned down in 1871 and been reconstructed on a much larger scale in less than twenty years. Its prodigious growth in population and business was Chicago's claim to fame, but at the same time these achievements deflected more meaningful recognition. In the opinion of those who resided in older cities on the East Coast, Chicagoans were certainly successful in making money, but they failed to do anything significant with it; Chicago was considered to be a city of commerce, not of culture.[4] Its art museum, symphony, opera, and theater were still very young and were not awarded the high stature of similar institutions in New York or Boston.

A new generation of Chicago businessmen, who had taken over their fathers' businesses in the 1880s (Charles L. Hutchinson, Martin A. Ryerson, Edward E. Ayer, and Franklin MacVeagh, among others), were clearly bothered by Chicago's second-class status and expended considerable energy trying to change the East Coast clichés about Chicago. They constituted a cultural elite that spent a great deal of attention and money on Chicago's cultural institutions.[5] They also supported their city in its fight with Washington, St. Louis, and especially New York to bring the world's fair to Chicago in 1892, and they contributed a large portion of the ten million dollars necessary for this purpose.[6] These men felt that if Chicago succeeded in their endeavor, East Coast skepticism could be overcome.

In early 1890, after a fierce battle in which Chicago was repeatedly forced to defend itself in attacks against its provincialism, the U. S. Congress determined that Chicago should host the world's fair. This decision represented a great boost for Chicago; yet, until the World's Columbian Exposition opened on May 1, 1893, the city's sense of inferiority about its supposed lack of culture remained. Architecture was one field in which this issue came to the fore. *The Inland Architect and News Record*, for example, noted that a sketched design for an art building at the fair, made by John Root shortly before he died in early 1891 (right around the time when he, Daniel Burnham, Frederick Law Olmsted, and Henry Codman were designing the layout of the fair), had to be realized despite the architect's death because "its abandonment would show that there is truth in the belief too common in the East, that Chicago has no true art sentiment, but is thoroughly commercial in her instincts."[7] Apparently, Chicago's achievements in architecture had not yet convinced the East Coast critics that the city had an architectural culture. Well-designed buildings for the display of art, such as the one by Root, apparently possessed the potential to change people's perceptions about this city; exposition halls and their contents could reasonably be expected to produce the same result.

It was within the context of these feelings of inferiority—the United States vis-à-vis Europe, and Chicago vis-à-vis the East Coast—that the design of the World's Columbian Exposition's fairgrounds and buildings took place. Only by approaching the fair's design from the perspective of the debates raging during the 1890s about national unity and American civilization can it be fully understood.

Before his death in early 1891, John Root designed a building to display art at the fair. Many historians assumed for a long time that, had Root lived, the fair would have followed Root's Romanesque style.

The first discussions about the design of the fair took place even before Congress had designated Chicago as the fair's host. These discussions, begun in 1889, were in response to the world's fair in Paris at the time. The participants were motivated by a desire to outdo this European precedent by creating an American fair, the grandeur of which would prove that American culture was not only equal to, but had surpassed European culture.

The Paris Exposition Universelle, organized to commemorate the centennial of the French Revolution, was the fourth world's fair held in the French capital and was tremendously successful in terms of the number of visitors it attracted and the profit it generated. Although less than one-third the size of the fair organized in Philadelphia in 1876, the Exposition Universelle was the largest fair ever held in Europe, attracting four times as many visitors as the Philadelphia fair. The visitors to the 1889 fair were impressed by the technical innovations on display, especially Edison's phonograph, but what they liked most of all was the design of the fair buildings. All structures were built of metal and glass and, further testifying to the skills of French engineering, the fair's Halle des Machines boasted the largest single span ever built. The most popular structure was the Eiffel Tower, which, despite the initial disdain of many Parisians, became the symbol of the 1889 fair and of Paris. The tallest edifice in the world, it was regarded as a marvelous display of what modern engineering could achieve.

The desire to outstrip Paris in both quality and size played a prominent role in the thinking of Chicagoans when they began to talk about hosting a fair. It was only after Paris had opened its splendid fair that Chicagoans became serious about host-

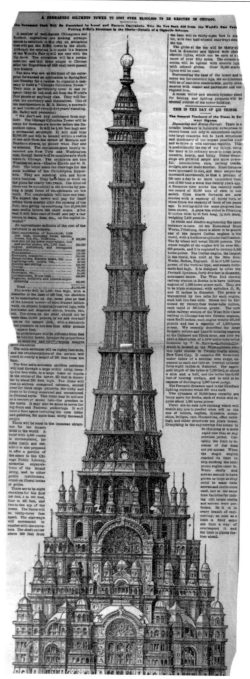

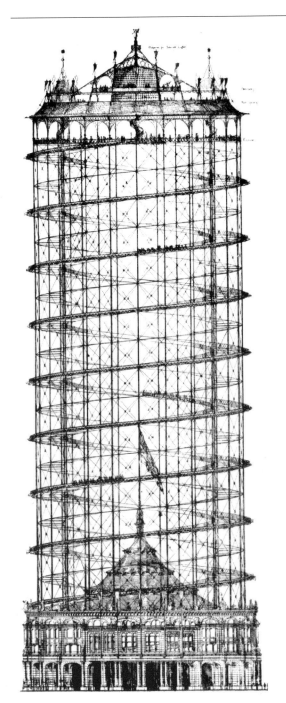

ROOF PLAN

FLOOR PLAN.

In their attempts to emulate the 1889 Paris fair, Americans developed many schemes for towers that would surpass the Eiffel Tower (far left), both in height and in cost. Examples are, from left to right, the Columbus Tower by Washingtonians Charles Kinkle and G. R. Pohl, the Johnstone Tower by Danish-American architect Alfred Roewade, and the Columbian Memorial by Chicago architect C. M. H. Vail.

ing a world's fair.[8] After 1889, references to the Paris fair appeared frequently in debates about its projected counterpart in Chicago. In September 1889, for example, when George Pullman bought one hundred thousand dollars of stock in the Chicago enterprise, he claimed, "It will undoubtedly be the greatest exhibition this country has seen and there is no reason why, with three years in its favor, it should not eclipse the Paris centennial."[9]

That Chicagoans sought to rival Paris in shaping their own fair is evident in the numerous sketches of towers printed in the *Chicago Tribune* in October and November of 1889. The newspaper had asked private citizens to submit designs that would show that Chicago could surpass the Eiffel Tower and the 1889 fair. All of these designs were reminiscent of the Eiffel Tower, yet taller, without paying too much attention to the structural aspects of such a tower. Although the *Tribune* announced in late November 1889 its decision "to close the gates on the designers of world's fair towers," people's imagination had been stirred, and more serious proposals continued to be discussed in the newspaper. In May of the following year, a headline in the *Tribune* announced: "A Permanent Columbus tower to cost over $2,000,000 to be erected in Chicago." The first sentence of the article declared that the tower designed by Washington, D.C., residents Charles Kinkle and G. R. Pohl would "put the Eiffel Tower in the shade."[10] Intended to stand fifteen hundred feet (some six hundred feet taller than the Eiffel Tower), the projected steel and cast-iron structure looked like a strange mixture of the Eiffel Tower rising over a base inspired by San Marco Cathedral in Venice.

Other kinds of structures were proposed for the purposes of outdoing the Eiffel Tower and representing the entire fair. Top left, the Hollingsworth Hemisphere and, bottom left, the Columbus Egg-Shaped Building. The Proctor Steel Tower (Holabird and Roche, 1891), left, was the only proposal that had a realistic chance of being built. This plan, however, was also cancelled.

The legacy of the Eiffel Tower haunted the Chicago fair to such an extent that the two became virtually inseparable. In early 1890, E. S. Jennison, for example, proposed to house the entire fair in a single gigantic, tent-like structure of metal and glass surmounted by a tower. Similar in design was the proposal by C. M. H. Vail, "a rising young architect in City Hall," for a Columbian Memorial tower. Described as an "absolutely original and unique design," this tower's height and shape were determined by symbolical references to Columbus and his voyage, rather than by structural considerations: it was supposed to stand 1492 feet tall on top of a metal and glass dome, which rested on a structure in the shape of an eight-pointed star.[11] The press published many other building designs that were not towers but nevertheless addressed the power of the Eiffel Tower as a symbolic image that had to be rivaled in whatever monument would finally be chosen to symbolize the Chicago fair. Several of these proposals dealt with the theme of Columbus exploring the world, embodied in buildings in the shape of a globe. The most remarkable designs were the Columbus Egg-Shaped Building, by architects Worthmann and Neebe, and The Hollingsworth Hemisphere, a structure shown floating in Lake Michigan and containing part of, perhaps even the entire, fair.[12]

Rivaling Paris by building a tower larger than Eiffel's remained a cherished dream. The project with the best potential for realizing that dream was the so-called Proctor Tower, designed in 1891 for inventor David Proctor and the Columbian Tower Company by Chicago architects Holabird and Roche together with the engineer Corydon T. Purdy. The architects planned to place this tower in the Court

of Honor on a strip of land between the Grand Basin and Lake Michigan, a site commensurate with the location of the Eiffel Tower in the 1889 fair's Court of Honor at the edge of the River Seine. This initial plan was soon relinquished by the World's Columbian Exposition's team of architects and landscape architects in favor of providing a more monumental enclosure for the Court of Honor: a series of thirteen columns symbolizing the first thirteen states of the Union.[13] The tower was then moved to the back of the Woman's Building, where it marked the border between Jackson Park and the Midway. In the end, however, after the foundations had been laid, plans for the Proctor Tower were canceled, probably for financial reasons. Instead, George W. G. Ferris won the concession to construct his Ferris Wheel at the center of the Midway. In certain respects like a tower, this 250-foot revolving wheel also functioned as a lookout point, and, like the Eiffel Tower in Paris, it eventually came to symbolize the Chicago fair.[14]

Though the effort to rival specific structures seen at the 1889 Exposition Universelle was ultimately not realized, the World's Columbian Exposition did, in fact, far surpass its Parisian precedent in the dimensions of the site and the size of the buildings. The Chicago fair covered a surface of 686 acres, while the Paris fair covered only 72 acres.[15] The major buildings around the World's Columbian Exposition's Court of Honor were gigantic. For example, the largest building, dedicated to Manufactures and Liberal Arts, measured 787 by 1687 feet, while the Halle des Machines, the largest structure at the Paris fair, measured about 330 by 1270 feet. Chicago's Machinery Hall and Agriculture Building had annexes that almost doubled the size

of these buildings, so that Machinery Hall, for example, measured about 490 by 1393 feet. Indeed, the World's Columbian Exposition in general and the Court of Honor in particular were so impressive that the writer Henry B. Fuller had no trouble deciding which fair was more impressive: "We are then ready to ask how the great spectacle thus formed compares with that seen from the Eiffel tower . . . for Chicago will compare herself with only the latest, the biggest, the best. And in this case the comparison need not be feared. . . . For the buildings at Jackson Park are much more numerous than

The Halle des Machines was the largest structure at the 1889 world's fair in Paris, but was much smaller than Chicago's Manufactures and Liberal Arts Building, which measured 787 by 1,687 feet. Inside both buildings looked almost identical.

26.

those of the Champs de Mars, much larger, much more splendid individually and much more overwhelming in their associated effect."[16]

While the sense of inferiority the United States felt vis-à-vis Europe resulted in an effort to outdo the Paris world's fair of 1889, the competition between Chicago and the other cities vying for the fair resulted in a desire on the part of the organizers to create a world's fair that would represent the entire nation and not just one city. In the debates pitting New York against Chicago, one argument was raised repeatedly: Chicago was too provincial to host the fair. New Yorkers tried to convince Congress and the rest of the nation that a world's fair in Chicago would achieve no more than a county fair. They argued, for example, that a fair in the Midwest could not attract international business and would, therefore, be limited to displaying cattle and locally produced agricultural implements, a showing that would not present an appropriately diverse picture of American society to the world at large. Chicago responded to these attacks by pointing to citizens' remarkable efforts at rebuilding the city after the Great Fire of 1871. Chicagoans' energy and spirit were fundamentally American, and, therefore, Chicago was perfectly capable of representing all of America and its culture. Another compelling argument pointed out that Chicago was the hub of the vast midwestern region whose huge population lacked the means to travel to New York but would welcome the opportunity to visit a nearby fair. New York's boosters argued that their city should host the fair because it was the gateway for European visitors entering America; Chicago countered that it was also a gateway—a gateway to the many people in the vast plains. Moreover, a fair in Chicago

would give European visitors a chance to see more of the country. Chicago's mayor, DeWitt C. Cregier, eloquently remarked in presenting the case for Chicago to Congress: "Remember the thousands of square miles that lie on the other side of the Alleghenies; remember the great chain of lakes; remember St. Louis, the mistress of the world's greatest rivers; remember all these things, and let New York with her greatness always in the fore, not forget that she is circumscribed, and that she must depend for her future progress and her greatness—not altogether, gentlemen, but largely—on those fertile miles and acres in the West."[17] The monthly journal, *The World's Columbian Exposition Illustrated*, boasted more succinctly: "As it was true of old, that all roads lead to Rome, it is equally true now that all roads lead to Chicago."[18]

The claim of representing the large midwestern states enabled Chicago to win the battle for the fair, which was finally decided by Congress in April 1890. Winning the battle did not mean, however, that fears of provincialism had been overcome. Congress decided to monitor the organization of the fair and created a national commission of prominent men in the country (two from each state) to approve the fair site, building plans, classification of exhibits, allotment of exhibit space, and appointment of exhibit judges. The commission's president was Thomas W. Palmer, a former senator from Michigan and, appropriately for a Columbian celebration, former ambassador to Spain. On a local level, Chicago set up the Chicago Corporation to oversee selecting the fair site, raising funds, constructing the buildings, and operating the fair.[19]

The existence of a national as well as a local board may have created some inefficiencies, but it

The fair allowed Chicago to claim a position for itself as a leading cultural city, as the "Metropolis of the West." This claim was substantiated by the fair's architecture, as well as by publications.

Opposite, Machinery Hall. Photograph by W. H. Jackson. Above, Chicago of To-day: The Metropolis of the West.

did allow those outside Chicago to feel they retained some control over how America would be represented at the fair. For example, the issue of what the fairgrounds and buildings should look like—the foremost criterion by which the fair would be judged—was a concern of both the national and local boards. Chicago's Committee on Grounds and Buildings appointed the architects who would design the fair buildings, but, as the plans proposed by these architects needed the approval of the national commission, it made sense to appoint architects who represented the entire country.

The selection of the architects was made in late 1890 by Daniel H. Burnham, a prominent Chicago architect. In 1889, long before Chicago was selected as the city to host the fair, Burnham had gotten involved with the organizers of the fair as an adviser on architectural matters.[20] It has never been documented why Burnham rather than some other prominent Chicago architect (Holabird and Roche or William LeBaron Jenney come to mind) was invited to assist the fair organizers at such an early stage, but there are some obvious reasons. First, Burnham may have known several of the fair's early organizers well, although none of them

had used Burnham as an architect.[21] By 1889, moreover, Burnham and his partner, John W. Root, had a well-established architectural firm that, over the fifteen years of its existence, had slowly developed into one of Chicago's most important high-rise office builders. Their buildings included major achievements such as the Montauk Building, the Rookery, and the Monadnock Building. Together with the firm of Holabird and Roche, Burnham and Root shared the distinction of being the leading architectural firm in the city.

Burnham's early interest in the fair was rewarded in September 1890, when he and John Root were formally appointed as consulting architects by the Committee on Grounds and Buildings. Later that year, Burnham became chief of construction, and Root was appointed as supervising architect. The Committee on Grounds and Buildings left it up to Burnham to determine if he wanted to hire other architects for the project and, if so, to select them.

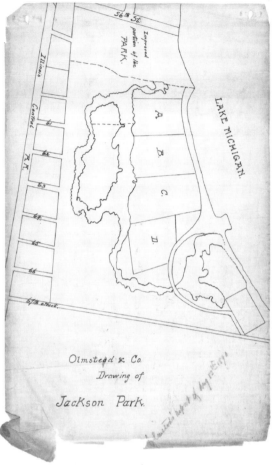

Before the fair, Jackson Park, c. 1890, consisted of sand dunes and swampland. Olmsted proposed to make the higher elevations of Jackson Park, which were covered with native oak trees intermingled with bushes, into platforms for buildings and the swampy areas into waterways. This drawing of August 1890, above, is the first proposal for the creation of an island and a continuous body of water.

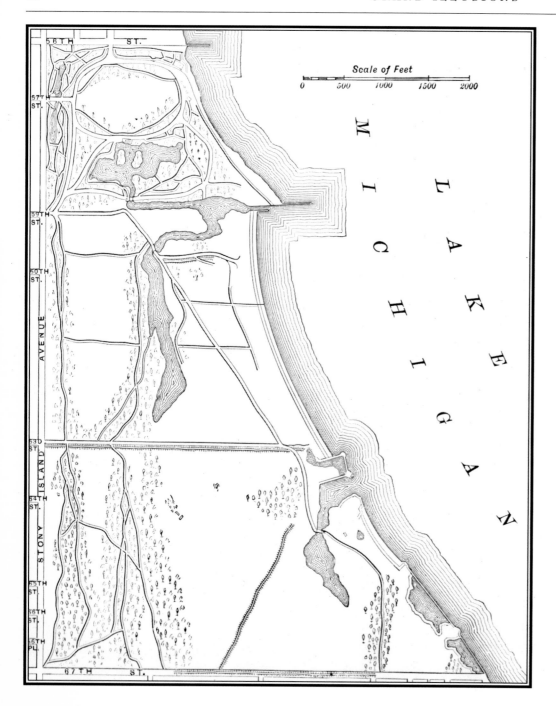

Before Burnham could make any appointments, a general plan, including square footage of the buildings, had to be worked out. Burnham and Root worked on this plan with the well-known landscape architect Frederick Law Olmsted and his assistant Henry S. Codman, who were appointed as supervising landscape architects in late November. By that time, a protracted battle over the site of the fair had finally been concluded in favor of Jackson Park and Lake Front Park, where a few buildings, such as the Fine Arts Building, would be constructed.[22] At the same time, the national commission approved a classification system—a system that divided all products to be shown at the fair into a number of categories, thus determining which product would be shown in which building—as well as a rough estimate of square footage needed for each category within this classification.

Burnham, Root, Olmsted, and Codman together devised a layout for the fair, which was approved in December 1890 by both the national commission and the Chicago Corporation. The basic characteristics of the final plan can already be recognized in this early plan: the Court of Honor surrounded by five major exposition halls and another body of water, the lagoon, with a large island in its center.

With the general plan approved, Burnham had to decide whether to appoint other architects to design buildings for the fair. He recognized that the project was too large and complex to be handled by a single office. In a lengthy report, dated December 9, 1890, and addressed to the Committee on Grounds and Buildings (the body that had to approve Burnham's selection), Burnham declared that he was absolutely against a competition because the best architects would not want to spend time creating a

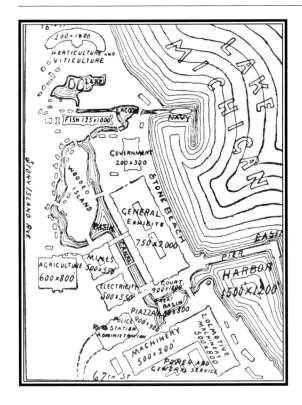

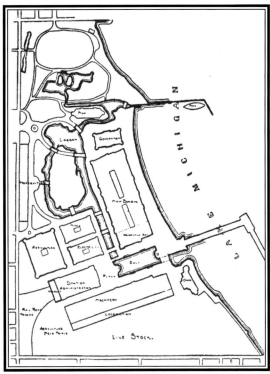

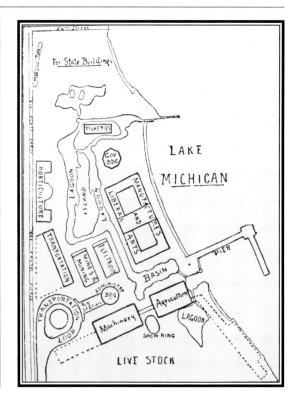

design that risked rejection, and any competition would, therefore, result in mediocre plans. On these grounds he sought permission to commission buildings outright from a certain number of architects.[23] Burnham's proposal was accepted by the committee, which then assigned him to select five architects to design the buildings on the Court of Honor at the heart of the fair. The architects Burnham chose were Richard Morris Hunt, McKim, Mead and White, and George B. Post, all of New York, Peabody and Stearns of Boston and Van Brunt and Howe of Boston and Kansas City.

This selection, in which no Chicagoan was included, has provoked a great deal of commentary. Several historians have interpreted Burnham's

choices as an expression of a sense of inferiority on his part, arguing that he did not think Chicago architects could live up to the gigantic task of designing the fair. The few relevant documents written by Burnham during and after the fair, however, clearly indicate that the selection was intended to enable the fair to become truly national in scope and character.[24]

In his December 9, 1890, report to the Committee on Grounds and Buildings, Burnham alluded to this argument when he spoke of the impact of good design on America's reputation in the world; in other words, the fair was an American enterprise according to which the whole nation would be judged. The buildings should be "of the highest

The design for the fair-grounds was refined between November 1890 and early spring 1891. The dates of the designs here illustrated are (from top left): November 1890, December 1890, and January 1891.

Opposite: Jackson Park before the fair.

possible architectural merit." Selecting architects from outside Chicago guaranteed that the fair would not be local, but instead national in character: "The results achieved by them will be the measure by which America, and especially Chicago, must expect to be judged by the world."[25]

In other speeches and writings, Burnham indicated that it was his desire and the committee's intention to bring together the "best artistic talent in the country without regard to residence."[26] Yet the question remains why he considered East Coast architects to be the most talented. One part of the answer might be that Richard Morris Hunt, the first American trained at the Paris Ecole des Beaux Arts, was generally considered to be the dean of American architecture. Hunt's national stature made him a candidate for the position of consulting architect for the fair, the position for which Burnham and Root were ultimately chosen.[27] Why the committee decided against Hunt is not clear—perhaps because of his relatively advanced age (he was sixty-three years old at the time), or because the committee members recognized the substantial advantage of appointing a consulting architect who was based in Chicago and, therefore, readily available. In any case, it seems clear that, from the beginning, planners believed the fair should represent the whole nation. Hunt's name and those of his East Coast colleagues might have surfaced repeatedly as possible designers; at the time Root was secretary of the board of the American Institute of Architects, and he must have frequently interacted with Hunt, who was president. Furthermore, Hunt was also a good friend of Frederick Law Olmsted, the fair's consulting landscape architect. Olmsted was working with Hunt on the Biltmore in Asheville,

North Carolina, an enormous, chateau-like summer mansion for George W. Vanderbilt. Yet another reason for the prominence of Richard Morris Hunt and his East Coast colleagues may be found in *The Inland Architect and News Record*, which reported in September 1890 that Burnham and Root were considering building the fair in the three most popular styles in the country at the time: Romanesque, Francis I, and colonial.[28] The fair could, therefore, be considered distinctly American. Each of the East Coast architects chosen had built a major structure in one of these styles, which may have been the rationale for Burnham and Root to invite their participation in planning the 1893 fair.[29]

Once the five architects had accepted the invitation to work on the major buildings, Burnham wrote to the Committee on Grounds and Buildings in terms that underline the importance of the fair's architecture in securing the exposition's national stature: "You have removed all doubt as to Chicago's attitude toward the entire country, and have secured the cordial approval of architects everywhere."[30] The press, too, was informed that the need to endow the fair with a national rather than a regional character provided the rationale for selecting East Coast architects, and this information was duly published in Chicago newspapers. On December 13, 1890, the *Chicago Tribune* reported that the honor of being selected "could not fail to be productive of a result which would stand before the world as the best fruit of American civilization." A few months later, the *Chicago Times* made much the same point: "The best architects in the country prepared the plans for several buildings and the structures they have designed will exhibit the highest achievements of American architecture."[31]

Top to bottom: Charles F. McKim, Solon S. Beman, George B. Post, Louis H. Sullivan, and Richard M. Hunt.

Opposite: The Manufactures and Liberal Arts Building by George B. Post and the Agriculture Building by McKim, Mead and White seen from across the South Canal. Photograph by C. D. Arnold.

Not everybody on the committee was receptive to Burnham's choice of East Coast architects to design the fair's most important buildings. Ferdinand W. Peck and Potter Palmer, who had both worked extensively with Chicago architects and may have even been prompted by the architects with whom they had worked before,[32] protested vehemently against Burnham's selection and demanded that Chicagoans be represented in the design of the fair. In his forceful response, Burnham exploited his standing as an accomplished and respected architect, saying that what was at stake was "not a question of men, but of Art" and that his knowledge about this matter together with his professional expertise ought to carry more weight than the opinions of laymen on the committee.[33] Although Burnham retained the authority to appoint architects, he was nonetheless asked by the Committee on Grounds and Buildings to submit a list of ten Chicago architectural firms, from which he chose five firms to design major buildings outside the Court of Honor. These firms were Adler and Sullivan, William LeBaron Jenney, Henry Ives Cobb, Solon S. Beman, and Burling and Whitehouse. Why these particular firms were selected is not clear, but connections between them and Burnham or Root may have played a role.[34] With this selection of the best architects from the East Coast and the Midwest, the committee of architects had become truly national in character.

These architects were commissioned to design a fair that would tell the world that the American states composed a single nation united under one government. The means determined by the architects to achieve this goal were unity in style and dimension. Even before the first meeting of the ten architects in Chicago on January 10, 1891, the New York contingent had met and decided (without Burnham being present) to adopt the classical style for the buildings around the Court of Honor. This decision, even more than Burnham's selection of New York architects, has been blamed as the source of an abiding conservatism in American architecture and as the evidence of the overwhelming power of the Ecole des Beaux Arts in the United States. Overlooked in the rush to condemn this so-called return to historicism is that these architects had a specific reason for choosing a common style. If the Court of Honor, which they were commissioned to design, was to be the centerpiece of the whole world's fair, and if this centerpiece had to convey the message that the fair represented a unified nation—despite the country's diverse population and recent civil war—then all the buildings should be designed in the same style to embody the concept of unity. To strengthen the harmonious effect of a single style, the architects decided to adopt a common cornice height of sixty feet and a modular bay width of twenty-five feet. The unity thus achieved in style, height, and width is what made the Court of Honor so stunning. The end result was a work of great harmony. As Henry Van Brunt, one of the architects who worked on the Court of Honor, eloquently noted: "In this vast orchestra, no individuality forces itself into undue prominence to disturb the majestic symphony."[35]

Because the European world's fairs functioned as the salient model for those planning the World's Columbian Exposition, one might expect to find that the East Coast architects had imitated the metal-and-glass structures used in Europe. The advantage of those buildings, as Paxton had shown with his Crystal Palace for the first world's fair in London in 1851, was that they could be con-structed in a very short time, since most of the structural elements could be standardized and pre-fabricated. The New York architects' lack of experience with these techniques prevented them from working in this style, which Hunt condemned in a speech to the annual convention of the American Institute of Architects for not having produced any satisfactory designs to date. "The last two French expositions showed great merit in the adaptation of iron to architectural effects, but much yet remains to be accomplished before the artistic mind will be satisfied."[36] Instead of metal and glass, Hunt said, the architects preferred a more dignified, classical style. He failed to mention, however, that the structural parts of the main exposition halls (the steel and wooden arches and trusses) were actually very similar to those used in Paris and at other recent fairs, and that the classical facades were no more than plaster masks that rendered these structural features invisible.

Many architectural historians have suggested that the classical style used in the Court of Honor was the only one available to the New York architects, whose choices were severely limited by their beaux-arts training. If one examines the total oeuvre of these architects, however, it becomes evident that the classical style was not featured in most of their other work. Richard Morris Hunt, for example, employed either a late medieval or an early Renaissance style for his residential and office buildings; only for the most monumental structures did he resort to a classical style. Henry Van Brunt's work included many styles, as did the work of Peabody and Stearns. McKim, Mead and White were perhaps the only architects in the group who consistently employed beaux-arts classicism.

Markedly different in appearance from the other fair buildings, Louis Sullivan's Transportation Building received mixed reviews from contemporary critics. The most positive comment came from the French Union Centrale des Arts Decoratifs, which asked Sullivan to donate a plaster cast of the ornament to its museum. Photograph by C. D. Arnold.

28.

In early 1894, architectural critic Montgomery Schuyler gave several practical reasons for the stylistic choice made by the New York architects.[37] First, he noted, the classical style was part of the East Coast architects' training, whether at the Ecole des Beaux Arts in Paris or in the studios of architects who had been trained at that school. As all five architects knew how to design architectural details in this style, its use would make the achievement of unity easier than if four architects had to adjust to one other architect's idiosyncratic style. Second, Schuyler argued, the classical orders had lost their original meaning of supporting the roof of a structure and they could therefore be applied to any kind of building, even as an envelope around simple open halls without having to support anything, as in the Court of Honor. The abundance of classical buildings to serve as models made it possible to design the fair buildings relatively quickly, which would not have been the case with a freer, more romantic style that called for more personal expression. Finally, Schuyler pointed out that a great deal of diversity was possible within the unified classical style. This diversity within unity contributed to the Court of Honor's success, as it allowed each architect to choose the version of classicism he preferred (Roman, French Renaissance, or Venetian, for example) and to create variations within the established style. What Schuyler did not mention, perhaps because he was too much part of his own time to see it, was that there was also an ideological purpose behind the choice of the classical style: to further America's desire to play a more substantial role in world trade and world politics. If the United States wanted to be taken seriously as a world power that could compete with the traditional power brokers such as Great Britain, France, and Germany, it would not only have to prove that it could act as one nation rather than a collection of immigrants, it would also have to overcome the perception that the United States possessed no culture or, at best, a conglomeration of cultures transplanted from Europe. The selection of the classical style was part of an all-embracing program through which the fair organizers sought to demonstrate that there was indeed an American civilization.[38]

For many people in the late nineteenth century, the notion of civilization implied progress. What secured the civilized character of a country was its continuous achievement of progress in every field: arts, technology, economy, and trade. Only so-called primitive nations did not make progress; they remained bound to old habits. Late nineteenth-century Americans, looking back at the history of their country, believed that progress was achieved only after the arrival of European colonists. In their opinion, Native Americans had made no effort to develop the land or take advantage of the wealth of available materials but instead had simply lived off what the land provided.

In this conceptual framework, Columbus was an important figure in American history. He was not simply the first European to arrive on the continent but the initiator of the extraordinary development that characterized the ensuing four hundred years. The concept of American history as a record of progress coincided with the desire of the United States to become a world power. The result was a world's fair that celebrated Columbus as America's supposed first historic figure and that concentrated even more on presenting four centuries of American achievement as testimony to this coun-

The World's Columbian Exposition celebrated the four-hundredth anniversary of Columbus's first voyage across the Atlantic. Saint-Gaudens's statue of Columbus setting foot on land, below, stood in front of the Administration Building.

Opposite: The Columbian Fountain by Frederick Mac-Monnies. Photograph by W. H. Jackson.

Americans in the late nineteenth century revered Columbus as a hero. The tapestry, Columbus Sighting America, *showed sailors kneeling in awe of Columbus and was displayed at the fair in the Manufactures and Liberal Arts Building.*

try's readiness to assume a leading role in the world. The fair further celebrated the success of imperialism, for, as the official historian of the World's Columbian Exposition, Rossiter Johnson, wrote, the fair would show "the whole world's progress in the arts of civilization, much of which never would have been accomplished but for the new life, new energy, and new genius that sprang into being with the opening of new lands."[39]

The earliest official documents announcing the World's Columbian Exposition left no doubt about the fair's real purpose. The congressional act determining that a world's fair would be held in Chicago in 1892 brought all the salient elements together in the first clause of the law; the fair would celebrate the four-hundredth anniversary of Columbus's journey, exhibit America's resources, and demonstrate the progress of civilization in the "New World." The foreword to the "First Draft of A System of Classification for the World's Columbian Exposition," written for the national commission by George B. Goode, assistant secretary of the Smithsonian Institution because of his expertise in international exhibitions, also addressed civilization, progress, and the quatercentenary as related issues. Goode wrote that the fair should be "an Illustrated Encyclopedia of Civilization" that would become "the best record of human culture in the last decade of the Nineteenth Century." Goode then added an important sentence: "If such is to be the character of the undertaking, it will be necessary to depart very largely from the traditional methods of previous exhibitions, which have been pre-eminently industrial." In other words, a fair that was more than a display of merchandise, a fair in which each product on display conveyed an idea, had never been

held before. Such a fair fulfilled a need specific to America in the late nineteenth century.[40]

The difference between traditional fairs and the one being planned for Chicago, according to Goode, was that each display should teach a lesson, or, in the terminology coined at the time, should be an "object lesson," one taught not so much through words as through material objects. By the late nineteenth century, the notion that inanimate objects could provide information about the group or society that had produced it had become quite popular in the educational and museum world.[41] A lesson taught by an object could be especially clear if that object were compared to one or more other objects produced by a different culture, which was precisely what Goode hoped would happen at the World's Columbian Exposition. The concept of learning by comparison was appropriate for world's fairs, as comparison was the basic activity on which world's fairs were built. The 1851 London world's fair was organized to enable British industrialists to compare their products with those from other countries and thereby determine whether British products were sufficiently attractive to compete on the European market. The comparison and competition generated by that fair continued to be the aim of similar events staged in the following years, and many expected a similar format for the World's Columbian Exposition. More than two years before the opening of the fair in Chicago, one magazine anticipated that the World's Columbian Exposition would be "a vast cosmopolitan university, where the nations will become voluntary pupils and the work of their handicraft serve as object lessons for the study and benefit of all. . . . The children of the East can meet with those of the North, South and West, and all can learn of the advancement and progress which his fellow man has made on his respective portion of the globe."[42] Through the abundance of materials on display at the fair, the visitor would learn about the status of various civilizations and, especially, the progress of American civilization. As Colonel Davis, the executive director of the World's Columbian Exposition, said in an address to Congress, the fair would "celebrate the opening of a hemisphere for the benefit of humanity, for the progress of civilization and the advance of Christian religion."[43]

Believing that the progress of civilization was evident in history, the planners of the World's Columbian Exposition wanted to include many displays with historical components. From the moment it became known that Chicago was going to host the fair, proposals for historical displays poured in. George B. Goode and his superior at the Smithsonian Institution, S. P. Langley, wrote that, in addition to a display examining the history of the Smithsonian and another display devoted to the natural resources of the United States and how they were used, "an attempt should be made to show the physical and other characteristics of the principal races of man, and the early stages of the history of civilization as shown by the evolution of certain selected primitive arts and industries." They suggested that transportation by land and water was an especially appropriate topic for such a display. Any means of transportation ever known should be shown, thereby making visible the enormous progress humans had achieved and, especially, America's contribution.[44] Others also considered transportation a topic capable of illus-

trating progress. In a letter to Daniel Burnham dated January 26, 1891, Frederick Law Olmsted suggested that in the lake and on the lagoon there should be a collection of birchbark canoes, "managed by Indians suitably trained, equipped and costumed for the purpose," Venetian gondolas, a copy of Columbus's caravel, and "an exhibition of various sorts of quaint, foreign water craft in contrast with our own." They were to include "Malay proas, catamarans, Arab dhows, Chinese sanpans, Japanese pilot boats, Turkish caiques, Esquimaux kiacks,

Replicas of Columbus's ships, the Niña, *the* Pinta, *and the* Santa Maria, *were built in Spain for the Chicago fair and sailed to New York, and from there to Chicago. Visitors to the fair could view them in the South Inlet.*

Boats from various parts of the world floated in the fair's waters, allowing visitors to compare different means of transportation. Right: A Japanese boat near the Fisheries Building. Photograph by C. D. Arnold.

Below: A Venetian sailboat in back of the Mines and Mining Building. Photograph by C. D. Arnold.

Opposite: One of the gondolas that carried visitors through the fairgrounds. Photograph by C. D. Arnold.

Alaskan war canoes, the hooded boats of the Swiss Lakes." Even though Olmsted said in a later letter that he would like to provide these boats "as objects of curiosity or decoration, and for the suitable furnishing of the waters," his remark that they should "contrast with our own" makes clear that Olmsted was also interested in the comparative study of objects. [45]

The decision to include an Anthropology Department in the fair emerged from the same rationale, to use history to demonstrate progress. Frederic W. Putnam, curator at the Peabody Museum and head of the fair's Anthropology Department, organized a large exhibition devoted principally to the life of America's original inhabitants, the Native Americans. The items on display were both anthropological (objects collected from Native Americans in North and South America) and archaeological (objects retrieved from archaeological digs at Native American sites). These displays enabled the visitor to compare old and new artifacts created by Native Americans and therefore to experience the evolutionary progress of these people. Implied in this exhibition was the idea that a comparison between the displays in the Anthropology Building and everything else at the World's Columbian Exposition would teach visitors how much wealth their country had reaped since colonization began. To reinforce this message and to demonstrate the positive influence of Western civilization on indigenous culture, Putnam placed a small number of Indian villages and an Indian school amidst copies of Aztec ruins from the Yucatan near the Anthropology Building. [46]

In addition to the Anthropology Department, several other sections of the fair included historical

components. The Woman's Building, for example, "illustrated the progress of women through four hundred years."[47] It housed displays of objects made by nineteenth-century women from Europe and the United States, as well as a display of women's work by Native Americans. The Columbian relics in La Rabida (a reconstruction of the convent in Palos, Spain, where Columbus had spent some time before his voyage) conveyed a similar message about the relationship between history and progress. The various anchors of Columbus's boats, the copies of letters, maps, and other artifacts supposedly used by the explorer, were displayed in La Rabida not only to celebrate Columbus as the "discoverer" of America and give substance to his historical journey, but also to suggest the great strides America had made in the intervening four hundred years.

The architecture of the fair's exposition halls was similarly conceived to display the progress of American civilization. Classical details, such as domes and columns, and ornaments, such as the sculptures on the Administration Building or the mural paintings on the Agriculture Building, linked the fair to classical Rome and to the Renaissance in Italy, Spain, and France, and thus endowed the buildings with the same respect that was generally felt for the old cultures from Europe. These stylistic references to European history and geography transformed the facades into object lessons about culture and tradition. They suggested to the visitor that these historical cultures were incorporated into American culture and that the value commonly attached to those cultures could now be invested in American culture as well. The architectural styles used in the fair buildings created the impression that America had built a civilization of its own by

In the Anthropology Building, above, objects collected from various tribes in North and South America were displayed in a manner that would encourage the visitor to compare these cultures and learn about evolutionary progress. One of these objects was a totem pole from the Northwest Coast of the United States, far right. Photograph courtesy of the Field Museum.

The Japanese mask, right, was displayed on the Midway, where visitors could view peoples of various cultures living in settings designed to resemble their homeland. Photograph courtesy of the Field Museum.

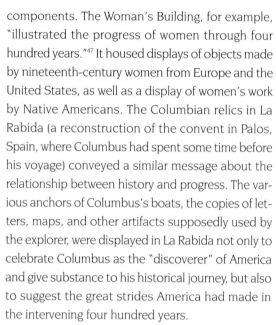

appropriating European traditions. In America, these styles could be interpreted more freely and on a scale not commonly experienced in their countries of origin.

The grandiose effects of these styles reinforced the measure of progress made by America. In the Court of Honor, history—in the guise of historical style—became an index of the maturity of American civilization; or, as Henry Van Brunt, the architect and critic declared: "The forums, basilicas, and baths of the Roman Empire, the villas and gardens of the princes of the Italian Renaissance, the royal courtyards of the Palaces of France and Spain must yield to the architects, 'in the new world which is the old,' their rich inheritance of ordered beauty, to make possible the creation of a bright picture of civic splendor such as this great function of modern civilization would seem to require."[48]

Van Brunt's statement makes clear why neither the Romanesque, Francis I, nor the colonial style was chosen, even though these were the most popular styles of the period and could have functioned as historical markers in much the same way as the styles that were chosen. The values attached to the Romanesque, Francis I, and colonial styles differed significantly from those associated with classicism. These styles lacked repose, or, in Van Brunt's terms, "ordered beauty." Moreover, these three styles were, because of the periods to which they referred, generally thought of as transitional, developing, or somewhat primitive. Historical references to the cultures that had produced them would not have suggested that the United States was part of a "modern," that is mature, civilization.

By demonstrating the sophistication of American civilization, the building facades around the Court

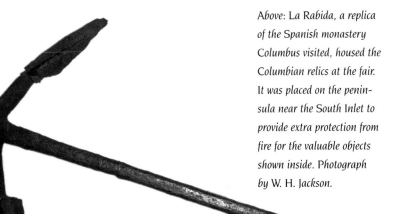

Above: La Rabida, a replica of the Spanish monastery Columbus visited, housed the Columbian relics at the fair. It was placed on the peninsula near the South Inlet to provide extra protection from fire for the valuable objects shown inside. Photograph by W. H. Jackson.

One of the objects on display here was the anchor supposedly from one of the ships used during Columbus's third voyage in 1498.

The classical ornament of the
Agriculture Building, above,
and Machinery Hall, oppo-
site, placed these buildings
in a long tradition going
back to Renaissance France
and Italy; there were, however, also some peculiarly
American elements on the

buildings, such as the
turkeys around the Agriculture Building's dome. Inside,
some pavilions, such as the
Ohio State Pavilion, right,
continued this reinterpreta-
tion. Its columns were of
glass filled with grains.

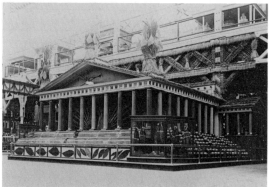

of Honor also validated the merchandise shown
inside these gigantic structures. Visitors entered the
major exposition halls after having seen the classical references on their facades, which, in the shape
of a thin layer of decorated plaster, enveloped the
buildings' interiors. This experience encouraged
consideration of the products available for inspection inside in a historical context. The interiors,
however, could not have differed more markedly
from the exteriors. These spaces were merely huge
sheds built with gigantic steel or wood trusses but
were completely visible. Here masses of products
were shown in exhibition stands—small, pavilion-
like structures that brought the gigantic size of the
buildings' interiors down to a more human scale—
all of which were designed by the companies spon-
soring the displays (or by designers hired by these
companies). As a result they lacked the formal unity
so characteristic of the exteriors. About the chaotic
appearance of the interior displays, Burnham
remarked in his *Final Report* that he wished he had
been responsible for supervising the design of the
displays as well as the buildings' exteriors. Such
control would have endowed the installations with
much greater artistic quality or, as Van Brunt would
have said, classical repose, than he believed they
actually possessed.[49]

In his *Book of the Builders*, however, Burnham indicated that it would not have been possible to design
the interiors in a manner similar to that of the exteriors: "It had been found early in the study of the
general design that it would be absolutely out of
the question to carry the construction of the
immense buildings to such a point that the interiors would harmonize with the facades either in style
or finish."[50] While lack of funds may have been one

reason for keeping the interiors bare of ornament, lack of time was probably another. It would have been neither economical nor efficient for the architects to design interior decoration and the construction workers to apply plaster walls and ornament in a building that would exist for no more than six months. Further, by the late nineteenth century, people were becoming accustomed to seeing products displayed in such vast, unadorned halls at world's fairs.[51] Visitors' attention may have wandered off sometimes to inspect the gigantic exposition halls, but in general it was drawn immediately to the displays in the exhibition stands. The buildings that did not show merchandise but that had a public function, such as the Administration Building, or displayed art, as did the Fine Arts Building and the Woman's Building, had finished interiors.

The architects themselves were the first to realize that, because their facades were no more than envelopes wrapped around structures created by engineers, the buildings did not constitute architecture in the fullest sense of that word. Burnham called the exposition halls "architectural sketches, carried out with sufficient elaboration and finish to give an effect of solidity and magnificence."[52] Van Brunt compared the facades to scenery "executed on a colossal stage, and with a degree of apparent pomp and splendor,"[53] further adding that all the beautiful architectural details were no more than "architectural screens" that had no function other than covering the building frames. In the same vein, Montgomery Schuyler called the fair "a success of illusion. . . . It was the task of the architects to provide the stage setting of an unexampled spectacle. They have realized in plaster . . . a painter's dream of Roman architecture."[54]

Behind its plaster classical facade, the Agriculture Building was a simple wooden structure, filled with small pavilions in which companies showed their products.

This illusion was created for a fair that was, first of all, a celebration of national unity and of American civilization. Celebratory architecture, such as the triumphal arches and stage sets built for pageants and parades, is temporary by nature and therefore very different from real architecture. Because of the fair's celebratory character, it was not too difficult for Chicago architects—who were strictly functional and businesslike in their designs for buildings in the Loop and claimed that there they made no direct reference to historical styles—to collaborate with the East Coast architects to design a fair with exposition halls in styles reminiscent of Roman or early Renaissance examples (Beman's Mines and Mining Building on the Court of Honor), or of Romanesque ecclesiastical structures (Louis Sullivan's Transportation Building and Henry Ives Cobb's Fish and Fisheries Building).[55]

In essence an illusion, the fair was never intended to be presented as a real alternative to the American city or, especially, to the city of Chicago. A great deal has been said during the past one hundred years about the contrast between the "White City" and the "Black City" (a name coined to distinguish Chicago from the fair and its white buildings) and about the fair as an urban ideal to which the actual city ought to aspire. The impact of the Columbian Exposition's splendor was, of course, great; many period descriptions in diaries and novels testify to the awe people felt. Yet the attraction of Chicago— the city that had been rebuilt in less than twenty years into America's second largest city; the city with the Masonic Temple, then the tallest building in the world; and the city of the gigantic Stock Yards— was equally great despite its less than pristine appearance. The fair and the city complemented

The exposed structural steel in Machinery Hall, bottom, reminiscent of a train shed, was appropriate to the objects displayed there. The companies displaying products in the Electricity Building, top, included Westinghouse and General Electric, whose Tower of Light, created with hundreds of incandescent light bulbs, was a major attraction. Photographs by C. D. Arnold.

After the fair, Burnham worked to transfer the design principles of the World's Columbian Exposition to the city. Burnham's proposal to build a bridge across the river at Michigan Avenue, opposite, and to extend this street north of the river

is one of the ideas presented in the 1909 Plan of Chicago that was realized. Painting by Jules Guerin. Above, proposal for Michigan Avenue from 1909 Plan of Chicago.

each other, much as the fair's exterior and interior architecture did. Visitors realized that the spectacle would not have been possible without the backdrop of the city and its complex realities.

After the success of the fair, however, Burnham began to concentrate on transfering its image of symmetry, unity, and civilization to the real city. He spent a great deal of time promoting a new plan for the American city based on the design of the

World's Columbian Exposition, but almost ten years passed before this concept received any serious consideration. In 1901, Burnham was invited to chair the McMillan Commission, which redesigned Washington, D.C., based on Pierre L'Enfant's plan of 1791. A few years later, the Commercial Club of Chicago commissioned Burnham to develop a comprehensive plan for Chicago, which resulted in his influential *Plan of Chicago* of 1909.

The new plans for Chicago and Washington initiated a nationwide movement—the City Beautiful movement—whose adherents sought to redesign the plans of many cities. Thanks to this movement, the fair's illusory notion of classical architecture as an expression of American civilization came quite a bit closer to reality. The Chicago plan, as well as the plans for Denver, Minneapolis, and San Francisco, imitated some formal aspects of the fair, particularly its axial layout. The use of axes and vistas was a significant change in the organization of the American city, which until the turn of the century had been laid out on a strictly rectangular grid in which each city block was equally important. Now, large boulevards that cut diagonally through the city grid and led to a civic center (as in the plans for Chicago and San Francisco) or to a cultural institution (as in Philadelphia) created a hierachy in which certain streets or parts of the city were more important than others. Such a change in city planning coincided with the United States assuming a greater role in world affairs and with a growing sense of confidence among Americans in the stature of their country. This confidence found expression in the prominence that the City Beautiful movement gave to architectural embodiments of government, not only on a national but especially on a local level, in the many civic centers designed (but not always realized) for cities all over the country in the early twentieth century. It is as if the fair's vision of classical grandeur and stability, produced in response to America's sense of inferiority, had, twenty years later in the City Beautiful movement, become entirely convincing, as if its plaster illusions could actually be transformed into concrete facts.

LOOKING THROUGH
THE ILLUSION

The World's Columbian Exposition was designed to instill a sense of national unity and propound the existence of a recognizable American civilization. These messages were conveyed not only by the classical styles of the buildings, but also by their decoration. The structures grouped around the Court of Honor carried most of the symbolism and ideology; other parts of the fairgrounds contributed to the program, though in less formal and metaphorical ways. The layout of the fairgrounds reveals that apparently disparate areas were in fact arranged to reinforce the lessons of the fair. The design of the fairgrounds and its buildings reveal the omnipresence of the fair's ideology.

According to Burnham's *Book of the Builders* (1894), the fairgrounds were divided into seven regions: the Court of Honor; the area immediately north of it, including the Wooded Island, the lagoon, and the buildings surrounding this body of water; the government area, consisting of the United States Government Building and the buildings for foreign nations; the area of the state buildings; the Midway Plaisance; the southeastern region, with such buildings as the livestock exhibition, La Rabida, and the Anthropology Building; and the warehouse and workshop area on the southwest side.[56] While Burnham and his collaborators undoubtedly found it useful to distinguish these sections of the fairgrounds, a glance at the map of the fair reveals three basic areas: Jackson Park was divided to comprise two of the components, while the Midway, attached to the west side of the park, formed the third. The northern part of Jackson Park was organized around a main axis that ran from north to south, parallel to the street grid on which the surrounding city of Chicago was constructed; the section south and east of the lagoon was arranged around a number of axes either parallel with or perpendicular to the shore of Lake Michigan. This axial shift enabled Olmsted, Codman, Burnham, and Root to emphasize the role of water in the contemporary visitors' experience, alluding to Columbus's historic voyage.

Before the construction of the fair started, the northern part of Jackson Park had already been developed as a park. As a result the Court of Honor, with its large buildings, was constructed on the south side of the park. To create the bodies of water in the fairgrounds, Olmsted made existing waterways deeper and used the excavated dirt to elevate other sections of the fairgrounds.

Opposite: Digging the Lagoon, *1891. Photograph by C. D. Arnold.*

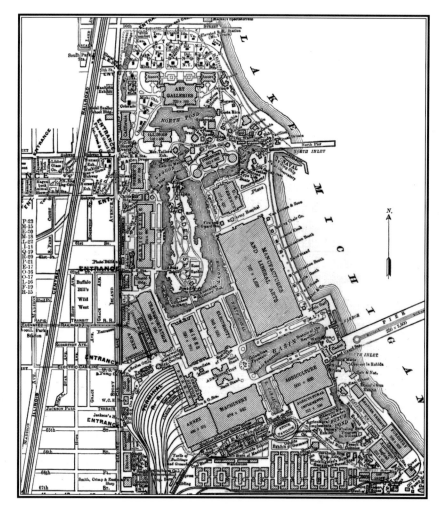

More than roads, water tied all the parts of the fair together. In the plan as it was realized, water connected the major buildings around the Court of Honor (each of which had at least one side facing the water) with the buildings around the lagoon and in the northern area around the Fine Arts Building. In fact, visitors to the fair could be moved across the fairgrounds by gondola or electric launch, and every building could readily be reached from the boat landings.

Water was already a plentiful feature of the undeveloped, marshy area Olmsted and his assistant, Henry S. Codman, saw in the summer of 1890 when they came to Chicago to look at Jackson Park. At that time, Olmsted decided to incorporate the water into the fairgrounds rather than eliminate it. In his earliest report to the Committee on Grounds and Buildings, written in autumn of 1890, Olmsted repeated a suggestion he had already offered to the South Park Commission almost twenty years earlier when, in 1871, he and his then-partner, Calvert Vaux, had first visited Jackson Park. Olmsted proposed that the fair organizers deepen low-lying parts of the park and turn them into water basins. The sand dug up in the process could be used to raise the higher areas of the park, thereby creating platforms to support the fair buildings. This concept for deploying the existing water, Burnham later acknowledged, was the only new idea behind the design of the fair. Speaking about the initial 1890 plan for the fairgrounds in a lecture to the World's Congress of Architects, Burnham admitted, "There was nothing original in it except the introduction of the canal, the lagoons and the wooded island; the grand court being the same arrangement as at Paris, with a waterbasin in the center and a dome at one end, in front of which was to be the great fountain."[57]

A view north from the Colonnade, above, allowed the fair visitor to look across the South Canal, Court of Honor, North Canal, Lagoon, and Wooded Island up to the State of Illinois Building. Around the Lagoon and Wooded Island, opposite, natural and man-made environments contrasted with each other. Photographs by C. D. Arnold.

With the exception of the Grand Basin in the Court of Honor, the placement of the water had an informal character that made the bodies of water appear to be natural; the placement of the buildings, however, was strictly axial and therefore formal in character. The use of two axes was an ingenious solution to the problem of relating the fair to the existing city on the one hand and to the lake on the other. Even in the first plan, published in November 1890, the buildings were oriented either strictly north-south or northwest-southeast.

The biaxial arrangement of the fairgrounds created a contrast between the formal and informal, the apparently natural and obviously man-made environments within the fair. The area aligned on the northwest-southeast axis was arranged symmetrically, thereby providing a sense of formality appropriate to the grand structures located there, including all the large exposition halls around the Court of Honor, as well as the Transportation Building, the Government Building, and the Fisheries Building. The formal quality of the northwest-southeast axis contrasted sharply with the rest of the grounds, which were laid out relatively irregularly and displayed more of the park's natural landscape. This informal area, arranged along the north-south axis, included the state and foreign government areas, plus the Fine Arts, Woman's, and Horticulture buildings, as well as the Wooded Island and the livestock exhibit.[58]

The roof of the Manufactures and Liberal Arts Building was a favorite lookout point. Looking north from this building one saw (right to left) the Government Building, the Fine Arts Building, the state buildings, and the Woman's Building.
Facing page: Many people came to the fair by boat and arrived at the pier, top, where a movable sidewalk took *them to the Peristyle, bottom left, a screen of columns that separated the lake from the Court of Honor. The triumphal arch in the Peristyle, bottom right, was a water gate into the fairgrounds, symbolizing Columbus's voyage across the ocean. The two parts of the Peristyle are connected by a bridge under the Triumphal Arch.*

The position of the Fine Arts Building in this biaxial arrangement is intriguing. Although its contents would arguably have justified a place on the Court of Honor, the Fine Arts Building was located in the northern part of the fairgrounds at a point where it could mediate between the "man-made" and the "natural" areas. This role was emphasized by the building's placement at the intersection of the two axes. The north entrance of the Fine Arts Building coincided precisely with the intersection of the north-south axis, and the axis that ran through the centers of the Fisheries Building, the United States Government Building, the Manufactures and Liberal Arts Building, and the Agriculture Building. The Fine Arts Building became the hinge where the two parts of the fairgrounds interlocked: through both the orientation of the building and its site, the Fine Arts Building was related to the fair's more natural environment; at the same time, the building's classical design (by the architect Charles Atwood, whom Burnham hired after the death of John Root in January 1891), asserted its relationship to the grand exposition halls that surrounded the Court of Honor.[59]

It may at first seem strange that the Court of Honor, the focal point of the design, was placed a great distance from the northern edge of the fairgrounds where people arriving by carriage or streetcar might enter. The northernmost part of Jackson Park had, however, already been developed as a park, and the South Park Commissioners (who owned the park) did not want the work they had accomplished there to be destroyed by a number of large exposition halls. Since the north side of Jackson Park was unavailable, Olmsted, Codman, Burnham and Root decided to place the Court of Honor almost at the southern edge of the park.

As a result of the fairground design, most people arrived at the fair either at the station in back of the Administration Building, or at the pier just east of the Court of Honor. Thus the Court of Honor became not only the focal point but also a spectacular "entrance hall" to the World's Columbian Exposition. In the latter case, visitors would walk down the pier and enter the Court of Honor, where they would be overwhelmed by the grandeur and splendor of the buildings and sculptural decorations. Those who arrived by train were also introduced to the court's splendor in stages. Emerging from the station, they arrived on a small plaza surrounded by the Administration Building, the Mines and Mining Building and Machinery Hall. The most logical way to proceed would have been to enter the Administration Building, admire its dome and mural paintings, and continue from there to the Court of Honor. From whatever direction a visitor entered the fair, she or he could not avoid the ideologically charged messages of America's progress and civilization conveyed by the grandeur of the Court of Honor.

The terminal station, left and below, was the entrance into the fair for those who came by train. Top photograph by C. D. Arnold.

Originally, the fair organizers had planned to place a series of thirteen columns, symbolizing the first thirteen states of the Union, to close off the vista towards the lake across the Court of Honor. Charles Atwood changed this design into the more solid Peristyle, left. Photograph by R. Capes.

The Statue of the Republic, right and opposite left, was designed by sculptor Daniel Chester French. Before the commission for this statue was given to French, the sculptor Augustus Saint-Gaudens, who advised the fair organizers about the selection of the artists, drew a sketch suggesting what a sculpture in the middle of the Court of Honor should look like, opposite right.

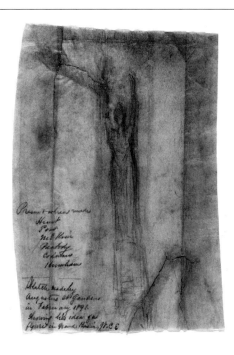

Within the space created by the facades, or "scenic screens" as Van Brunt described them, of the buildings around the Court of Honor, two pieces of sculpture stood out: the *Statue of the Republic* and the *Columbian Fountain*. Both works effectively embodied the concepts embedded in the fair. The *Statue of the Republic*, created by Daniel Chester French, towered over the court and, therefore, demanded immediate attention, all the more so because of the surface of gold leaf that covered the underlying plaster form. It was a colossal sculpture (standing sixty-five feet tall on a base forty feet high) of a woman holding a globe surmounted by a hovering eagle in one hand and a lance crowned by a Phrygian cap, a symbol of the French Revolution, in the other. The figure "symbolized both the republic of the United States, a single, united political entity, and our republican form of government."[60] Its archaic pose was, according to a contemporary observer, a response to "the almost perfectly symmetrical arrangement of the architecture about it,"[61] but it also signified the strength of a republic that had survived a civil war and was attempting to assimilate masses of immigrants from all over the world. The globe and eagle were the symbols chosen by the national commission for its official seal; here, however, the American eagle was shown hovering over the entire world, thereby alluding to the imperialistic aspirations of the United States. *The World's Columbian Exposition Illustrated* phrased it differently, suggesting that the *Statue of the Republic* invited "the nations of the earth to live under the form of government which our eagle symbolizes."[62] The Phrygian cap was used here as a symbol of the freedom that distinguished America from the rest of the world, an idea that continued to attract people to its shores.

COPYRIGHTED 189 BY C.D.ARNOLD.

The *Columbian Fountain*, designed by Frederick William MacMonnies, a student of Augustus Saint-Gaudens, stood in front of the Administration Building on the opposite side of the grand basin from the *Statue of the Republic*. This fountain, too, carried much symbolic meaning. While the *Statue of the Republic* referred to the country's government and the unity it had created among disparate people, the *Columbian Fountain* symbolized the nation and its aspirations. At the center was a barge steered by Time whose scythe was attached to the rudder, which consisted of a bundle of fasces, the symbol of authority in Roman times. The barge was rowed by female allegorical figures representing the arts, sciences, and industries. On the barge's prow stood Victory (sometimes called Fame) with a wreath in one hand and a trumpet in the other. Standing at the center of the barge were four putti supporting a throne on which Columbia, an allegorical figure symbolizing the country, sat with a torch in her hand while her feet rested on a globe.

The *Columbian Fountain* illustrated the progress made by America.[63] The barge stood for the ship of state, which, assisted by the arts, sciences and industries, had successfully led the country through the turbulent waves of time. The manner in which she was seated—not leaning back but bent slightly forward—was supposed to allude to America's eagerness for success. According to the architecture critic Henry Van Brunt, Columbia was "a fair, youthful figure, eager and alert, not reposing upon the past, but poised in high expectations."[64] The Victory figure standing at the prow told the viewer that Columbia's alertness had indeed enabled her to triumph.

The *Columbian Fountain* received wide acclaim. The architect Stanford White, partner in the firm of McKim, Mead and White, described it in a letter to MacMonnies as "awfully swell," even though he found the Victory "too skimpy about the legs and front drapery."[65] Because of the fountain's wide appeal, MacMonnies became better known to the public than any of the many other artists who created sculptures in the Court of Honor. To this day this work is more often referred to as the *MacMonnies Fountain* than as the *Columbian Fountain*.

After viewing MacMonnies's design for the Columbian Fountain, *opposite and above, Stanford White wrote to the sculptor: "St. Gaudens was so 'knocked over' by the enormous scale of everything in Chicago that he feared that the Boat and your figures would look small." Letter from Stanford White to Frederick MacMonnies, February 25, 1892. Photographs by C. D. Arnold.*

In addition to the *Statue of the Republic*, which personified national unity, and the *Columbian Fountain*, which represented the nation's ambitions, Columbus, the historical figure who initiated the country's progress, was also present in the Court of Honor. His statue stood atop the central portion of the Peristyle, which, since it was shaped as a triumphal arch, elevated both the act of entering the fair and the voyage of Columbus to the status of triumphal processions. Accordingly, the sculpture of Columbus showed the navigator standing triumphantly in a chariot pulled by four horses.[66] Texts inscribed in the walls of the arch clarified the importance of explorers such as Columbus. Names of explorers inscribed in the frieze over the arch were accompanied by odes that on the lake side (facing east, the direction from which the Europeans had come) were devoted to the explorers and settlers who had made America's development possible and on the court side to the "Pioneers of Civil and Religious Liberty," who had made America great. Civil liberty was described as "the means to build up personal and national character," and religious liberty as "the best fruit of the last four Centuries."

All together, the Columbus statue and the texts represented the victory of Western culture, which was reinforced (probably unconsciously) by the sculptures atop the columns of the peristyle and triumphal arch. This series of works consisted of multiple versions of an Orator, a Fisher Boy (both of which were Michelangelesque, classical statues), and a Native American (somewhat stiffer in stance and, on the basis of surviving photographs, apparently more archaic in style) that alternated with each other. The classical, Western tradition was clearly in the majority.

The sculpture on top of the triumphal arch in the Peristyle, right and opposite, showed Columbus as a triumphant emperor in a carriage pulled by four horses. Photographs by C. D. Arnold. The repeating statues on the Peristyle, above, represented an orator, a fisher boy, and a Native American.

Fire Controlled, *below,* and Water Controlled, *right, two of the sculpture groups by Carl Bitter for the Administration Building, opposite. Photograph by C. D. Arnold.*

Texts and sculptures on the other buildings similarly advanced both the purposes of those buildings and the intentions that motivated the fair. The Administration Building, for example, exhibited above each of its four doors a text recounting major episodes in Columbus's life. Its sculptures, symbolizing the triumph of mind over matter, signaled the progress of mankind. Sculptural groups on both sides of each of the four entrances showed one of the elements (water, fire, earth, and air) in its uncultivated state and in its cultivated state. For example, *Earth Uncontrolled* was shown through the figure of an old man, representative of a mountain, accompanied by a Paleolithic man standing on the head of a slain mammoth on one side and a woman fighting with an ape for some fruit on the other. Above this group, standing on a column, was a statue of the Goddess of the Harvest, symbolizing the powers in which "uncivilized man" believed. On the other side of the door, *Earth Controlled* was represented by figures who had cultivated the earth: a woman holding fruit and a crown of jewels, accompanied by a miner chiseling a rock to obtain the jewels and by a farmer boy carrying a basket filled with fruit. Towering above this group and standing on the column next to the door was a girl holding a basket of fruit. Other sculptures on the building symbolized virtues, such as tradition, abundance, and strength, that had helped the country progress.[67]

The architectural design of the Administration Building showed an interesting mix of styles, all of which were chosen for specific reasons. The four corner pavilions were similar in form and style to the other buildings around the Court of Honor: the height of their cornices were the same as those of

the neighboring buildings, and the arched windows had the same width as the windows on the other buildings. The second level was clearly inspired by the drum of the Capitol dome in Washington. The dome itself was vaguely modeled after Filippo Brunelleschi's fifteenth-century cupola of the Santa Maria del Fiore Cathedral in Florence. Thus, while establishing a stylistic unity with the other Court of Honor buildings, the Administration Building proclaimed its function of housing the fair management through a reference to the building that housed the country's policy-making body.

Only one building was systematically designed in one style: McKim, Mead and White's Agriculture Building, the style of which was generally described as purely Roman. Complementing its architecture, most of its sculpture and painted decoration were also inspired by examples from ancient Rome. The pediment over the main entrance, designed by Larkin Mead, brother of the architect William Mead, showed the *Return of Proserpina*, a classical myth explaining the yearly return of spring. Inside the first-floor arcades were murals directly inspired by the classical examples from Pompeii.[69]

The Mines and Mining Building, left, was the only building on the Court of Honor designed by a Chicago architect: Solon S. Beman. Photograph by C. D. Arnold.

Like the Administration Building, most buildings around the Court of Honor incorporated several classical styles, suggesting to the fair visitor many of the European cultures that contributed to American civilization. For example, the Mines and Mining Building by Solon S. Beman showed a mixture of Roman and Doric, as well as Italian and French Renaissance, Neo-Grec, and modern.[68]

The sculptural decoration on the pediment of the Agriculture Building, left, was chosen to illustrate myths related to farming. Photograph by C. D. Arnold. The Diana, goddess of the hunt, on top of the dome, opposite, was originally designed by Saint-Gaudens for Madison Square Garden in New York but was removed from there as it was too big. Photograph by W. H. Jackson.

Because of its Romanesque style, Louis Sullivan's Transportation Building has generally been considered strikingly different from the buildings located around the Court of Honor. Yet some of its details indicate that Sullivan was also thinking of his exposition hall as a building to illustrate progress in civilization. For example, the reliefs in the base of the Golden Arch (the main entrance into the building) illustrated the progress made in the field of transportation by showing ancient and modern transport modes. This concept of progress was highlighted by one of several inscriptions on the building: "Of all inventions—the alphabet and the printing press alone excepted—those inventions which abridge distance, have done most for civilization."

Louis Sullivan's Transportation Building, right, stood out among the fair buildings because of the intricate ornamentation and the bold use of color. Opposite top: One of the reliefs for the building by John J. Boyle illustrating the history of transportation. Photographs by C. D. Arnold.

The Ho-o-den Temple, above, integrated in the landscape of the Wooded Island. Photograph by George Glessner.

The symbolic meanings that were so abundant in the formally arranged part of the fairgrounds were absent in the less formal part. Yet it was the contrast between the formality of the Court of Honor and the informality of the rest of the fair that made the message of the Court of Honor so clear. The most informal part of the fair was the Wooded Island. Olmsted fought very hard to keep any planned intervention away from this island and to leave it instead to nature. He wanted the island to be a quiet place at the heart of the fair from which one could observe the entire fair. In his words, the island would "serve as a foil to the artificial grandeur and sumptuousness of the other parts of the scenery."[70] Olmsted's conviction was so strong that he even objected to the horticultural displays and the Japanese temple and garden that the fair organizers introduced to the island. Even though these displays barely intruded on the landscape, Olmsted felt that they damaged the island's purpose of presenting nature as pure and peaceful.

With the exception of some southern states plus Oregon and Nevada, all other states were represented at the fair, above. Photograph by C. C. Hyland. Popular amusements could be enjoyed on the Midway, opposite.

The area of the state and foreign nation buildings, the northern part of the fairgrounds, had already been developed as a park and could only be used for small buildings that would not drastically alter the landscape. The area looked, therefore, almost like a garden city. The diversity in building styles was appropriate for such a parklike setting. Yet, according to critics of the period, the region of state buildings was the least successful part of the fair; moreover, it contributed nothing to conveying the message of the fair. Montgomery Schuyler, for example, felt that the design of each individual building was adequate but that together they conveyed a chaotic image. He argued that this area should have been just as strictly planned as that of the Court of Honor.[71] Schuyler was clearly unaware that Burnham's office had devised guidelines for the design of the state buildings. These instructions required the designers to create each building in a style and material typical for the state.[72] Nobody, however, was responsible for coordinating these designs. Burnham's office played some supervisory role in the design of the state buildings, but this involved nothing more than overseeing the structural design; no aesthetic supervision was exercised. The lack of coordination and the resulting lack of unity in the state buildings emphasized the success of the East Coast architects who created unity among the buildings of the Court of Honor by coordinating their designs through the use of a common style, common cornice line, and common modular width.

The Midway was part of the overall design scheme for the fair only by default. Originally designed to receive overflow crowds in the event that Jackson Park would get too full, the Midway became the place where commercial concessions were located. These concessions consisted both of villages, built by people from various parts of the world (Egypt, Turkey, Java, Dahomey, etc.) who also sold merchandise and performed native dances there, and of attractions, such as the Ferris Wheel, the Captive Balloon, and the Ostrich Farm. Profiting from the knowledge that at the Philadelphia world's fair of 1876 all kinds of food and entertainment stands had lined the perimeter of the fairgrounds and thereby marred the appearance of the fair, the organizers of the Chicago fair decided to keep this aspect of the fair under control by confining it to the Midway. Each concessionaire was required to draw up a contract with the fair organization, in which the rights and duties of both parties were spelled out. The contract also indicated that the design of the buildings for any commercial attraction required the approval of the director of works, but, as was the case with the state buildings, Burnham exercised no control over the aesthetic aspect of the design; he inspected only the safety of the structure.

Yet as the locus of non-Western civilization and popular culture at the fair, the Midway had a specific function: to be the inverse of the image of American civilization presented at the Court of Honor. Indeed, the Midway was created to contain and to distance any features of the fair that might call into question the representation of American history and progress constructed in Jackson Park. There, the thin veneer of classical ornament and

architectural details over the large, open structures of the Court of Honor was complemented by the "natural" design of the Wooded Island and the areas north and west of it. Together, classical and natural design made up the fair's high culture, which, in turn, stood in contrast to the popular culture presented at the Midway.

In light of the striking coherence of the fair's interrelated physical components, from the decorative details of the buildings to the layout as a whole, it is clear that the architecture of the World's Columbian Exposition was more complex and meaningful than has previously been supposed.

Though never formally articulated, an architectural program existed, and the architects used the celebration of Columbus's voyage to promote a vision of American culture capable of rivaling the European model. While that model had been developed and refined over centuries, the version produced at the World's Columbian Exposition was constructed in only two years. Nevertheless, the World's Columbian Exposition created a grand illusion, through traditional cultural symbols, that satisfied Americans' desire for status and recognition as a unified nation.

NOTES

I would like to thank Connie Casey for her assistance with my research and for the many ideas she shared with me during our conversations about the architecture of the World's Columbian Exposition. This essay could not have been written without the support, patience, and advice of my wife, Nancy J. Troy; I am extremely grateful to her.

1. See "The Westward Route," in Alan Trachtenberg, *The Incorporation of America: Culture and Society in the Gilded Age* (New York: Hill-Wang, 1982), 11–37.

2. During the six months the World's Columbian Exposition was open to the public, a series of meetings, called congresses, was held in such fields as religion, architecture, history, and anthropology. Organized with the motto "Not Matter, But Mind; Not Things, But Men," the congresses discussed the progress in these fields and were thus an appropriate counterpart to the exhibitions at the fair that showed the material progress made by all the countries that displayed their products. Except for the Woman's Congress, which was held in the Woman's Building at the fairgrounds, all congresses were held in a building that, after the fair was over, became the Art Institute of Chicago.

3. H. Wayne Morgan, "Toward National Unity," in *The Gilded Age,* ed. H. Wayne Morgan, 2nd ed. (Syracuse, NY: Syracuse University Press, 1970), 9. See also Trachtenberg, *The Incorporation of America.*

4. See Helen Lefkowitz Horowitz, *Culture and the City: Cultural Philanthropy in Chicago from the 1880s to 1917* (Chicago: University of Chicago Press, 1989), 27ff.

5. See Horowitz, *Culture and the City,* 49–69.

6. The fair was originally planned for 1892. After Congress had chosen Chicago as the city that would host the fair (in early 1890), the decision was made to postpone the fair for one year until 1893.

7. "Progress in Columbian Exposition Work," *The Inland Architect and News Record* 17 (Feb. 1891), 1.

8. Fair proposals made by private citizens in newspapers or speeches in the early 1880s had not received enthusiastic response. See R. Reid Badger, *The Great American Fair: The World's Columbian Exposition and American Culture* (Chicago: Nelson-Hall, 1979), 46–49.

9. *Chicago Tribune,* Sept. 6, 1889.

10. *Chicago Tribune,* May 24, 1890.

11. E.S. Jennison & Co., *What Is the Proper Housing for an Exposition in 1893?* (Chicago: Shea Smith and Co., 1890). "The Columbian Memorial," clipping in John B. Kerfoot Scrapbooks on the World's Columbian Exposition, box "Clippings 1891," Chicago Historical Society Library.

12. "Riddle of Columbus, Design of an Egg-shaped Building for the World's Fair," in *Chicago Times,* April 18, 1891. "The Hollingsworth Hemisphere, A Floating Wonder for the World's Fair," in World's Columbian Exposition, Misc. Materials: invitations, cards, programs, etc., Chicago Historical Society Library.

13. The design for these columns by Augustus Saint-Gaudens was later replaced by a design for a triumphal arch and colonnade by Charles B. Atwood, which was eventually built as the Peristyle.

14. The Proctor Tower was closer to being a literal copy of the Eiffel Tower than any of the others proposed, yet there were several differences. Not only was the Proctor Tower supposed to be one hundred feet taller than its predecessor; it would also stand on six rather than four legs and have a central elevator shaft instead of elevators in each leg of the tower, thereby allowing for larger elevators to transport more visitors at a higher speed. Where the Eiffel Tower left its metal structure visible, the lower part of the Proctor Tower was supposed to be covered with ornament. All these differences ensured that the Proctor Tower would have a very distinctive appearance, despite the similarity of its silhouette to that of the Eiffel Tower. These circumstances clearly suggest that the designers wanted to emulate and outdo a Paris monument rather than create a monument to structural innovation. On world's fair towers, see Robert Jay, "Taller than Eiffel's Tower: The London and Chicago Tower Projects, 1889–1894," *Journal of the Society of Architectural Historians* 46 (June 1987): 145–56.

15. See Badger, *The Great American Fair,* Appendix A.

16. Henry B. Fuller, "Architecture and Decorations," in *The Chicago Record's History of the World's Fair* (Chicago: The Chicago Daily News, 1893), 88.

17. Mayor DeWitt C. Cregier in United States Senate, *Arguments before a Special Committee of the United States Senate by Hon. DeWitt C. Cregier, Mr. Thos. B. Bryan and Mr. Edward T. Jeffery in support of the Application of the Citizens of Chicago for the Location in their City of the World's Exposition of 1892* (Washington D.C.,: Government Printing Office, 1890), 4.

18. "The World's Columbian Exposition," in *World's Columbian Exposition Illustrated* 1 (1891): 2.

19. This corporation was led successively by Lyman Gage, William T. Baker, and Harlow N. Higinbotham. In order to streamline the collaboration between the national commission and the Chicago Corporation, an executive committee was installed by the national commission. Col. George Davis of Chicago became the director general.

20. Daniel H. Burnham, *The Final Official Report of the Director of Works of the World's Columbian Exposition,* reprint (New York: Garland, 1989); see also Charles Moore, *Daniel H. Burnham: Architect, Planner of Cities,* 2 vols. (Boston and New York: Houghton Mifflin Company, 1921).

21. Badger mentions as some of the early organizers: Andrew McNally, Lyman Gage, George R. Davis, George Pullman, Franklin Head, Edward T. Jeffery, Charles H. Schwab, Joseph Medill, and Mayor Cregier. See *The Great American Fair,* 49.

22. This plan was subsequently changed when it was decided that the entire fair should take place in Jackson Park. See Badger, *The Great American Fair,* chap. 8.

23. Judging from articles in *Inland Architect,* this sentiment against competitions was supported by most architects; see for example, "Progress of World's Fair Work at Chicago," *The Inland Architect and News Record* 16 (Aug. 1890): 1–2. For Burnham's report about competitions and selection of architects, see Daniel H. Burnham, "The Organization of the World's Columbian Exposition," *The Inland Architect and News Record* 22 (Aug. 1893): 6.

24. The first historian to mention this aspect was Titus M. Karlowicz; see "The Architecture of the World's Columbian Exposition," Ph.D. diss. (Northwestern University, 1965); and Titus M. Karlowicz, "D. H. Burnham's Role in the Selection of Architects for the World's Columbian Exposition," *Journal of the Society of Architectural Historians* 29 (Oct. 1970): 247–54.

25. This letter was published by Burnham in many different places, among others in his lecture, "The Organization of the World's Columbian Exposition," given at the World's Congress of Architects, and published in *The Inland Architect and News Record* 22 (Aug. 1893): 6.

26. See Daniel H. Burnham and Francis D. Millet, *The World's Columbian Exposition: The Book of the Builders* (Chicago: Columbian Memorial Publications, 1894).

27. "Appointment of Consulting World's Fair Architects," *The Inland Architect and News Record* 16 (Sept. 1890): 14–15. At this early time, the editor wrote also that Burnham's and Root's appointments had been met with approval from the profession, which assured the collaboration of the best architects in the country. See also Paul R. Baker, *Richard Morris Hunt*, 2nd ed., (Cambridge, MA.: The MIT Press, 1980), 395.

28. It may seem strange that the Romanesque and Francis I styles were mentioned as typically American styles. We should keep in mind, however, that with Romanesque is meant Richardsonian Romanesque, and with Francis I is meant the Loire-style architecture, as it was introduced by Hunt in New York. Both styles, derived from European examples, were developed by American architects.

29. It has often been suggested that the fair would have been different if John Root would have lived longer. This interpretation seems to be incorrect. John Root was involved in the selection of the East Coast architects and was described in the letter of confirmation that Burnham sent to the architects as the person who would work out their drawings without putting in his own feelings. In other words, Root would have made the working drawings of the buildings designed by Hunt and the other East Coast architects. It is impossible to imagine what Root would have done with the buildings he would have personally designed for the fair. His Romanesque design for a Fine Arts Building was intended to be placed in the Lake Front Park area. We do not know what Root would have done had he designed it for Jackson Park.

30. Daniel Burnham in a letter to the Committee on Grounds and Buildings, dated December 27, 1890, quoted in *The Final Official Report*, vol. 1, p. 6.

31. "World's Fair Work," *Chicago Times*, Apr. 26, 1891.

32. Ferdinand Peck had commissioned Adler and Sullivan to design the Auditorium Theater in 1886, and Potter Palmer, the real estate magnate and hotelier, had employed the architects Cobb and Frost for his own residence, and John M. Van Osdel for his Palmer House Hotel.

33. See Burnham, *Final Official Report*, part 1, vol., 1, p. 9.

34. Louis Sullivan was a very good friend of John Root and may have received support from Ferdinand Peck in the Committee on Grounds and Buildings; Jenney was Burnham's first employer in Chicago; and Cobb was a student of Peabody and Stearns and had his own proponent on the Committee of Grounds and Buildings, Potter Palmer. It is interesting that Holabird and Roche, one of the largest firms in Chicago at the time, was not included among these architects, even though they were on the original list of ten, together with Charles S. Frost, Treat and Foltz, Bauer and Hill, and J. L. Silsbee.

35. Henry Van Brunt, "The Columbian Exposition and American Civilization," *The Atlantic Monthly* 71 (May 1893): 583.

36. "President Richard M. Hunt's Address" (at the 25th annual convention of the American Institute of Architects, Boston, October 29, 1891), *The Inland Architect and News Record* 18 (Nov. 1891): 40.

37. Montgomery Schuyler, "Last Words about the World's Fair," *Architectural Record* 3 (Jan.–Mar. 1894): 291–301.

38. We should note here that the classical style had already been used as the official style since the American Revolution.

39. Rossiter Johnson, ed., *A History of the World's Columbian Exposition Held in Chicago in* 1893 (New York: Appleton, 1897–98), vol. 1, p. 2.

40. See also Robert W. Rydell, *All The World's a Fair: Visions of Empire at American International Expositions, 1876–1916* (Chicago: University of Chicago Press, 1984), 45.

41. On "object lesson," see Simon J. Bronner, "Object Lessons: The Work of Ethnological Museums and Collections," in *Consuming Visions: Accumulation and Displays of Goods in America, 1880–1920,* ed. Simon J. Bronner (New York: 1989),

42. "The World's Columbian Exposition," *World's Columbian Exposition Illustrated* 1 (1891): 2.

43. *World's Columbian Exposition Illustrated* 2 (June 1892): 70.

44. Appendix 7 to Report No. 890 of the House of Representatives, 51st Cong., 1st sess., March 1890. At the World's Columbian Exposition, there was indeed a display of the history of transportation in the Transportation Building. One of the artifacts displayed was the steam locomotive the Pioneer, the first train in Chicago, which is now in the Chicago Historical Society.

45. Letters from Frederick Law Olmsted to Daniel H. Burnham dated January 26, 1891 (this may be a mistake and may be 1892) and February 26, 1892. Library of Congress, container 38, WF file. I am grateful to Victoria P. Ranney for sharing this information with me.

46. The fair's Midway had in origin the same purpose of showing evolutionary development; however, under the direction of Sol Bloom, a young impresario, the Midway was turned into the fair's entertainment section. See Rydell, *All the World's a Fair*, 60–64.

47. Jeanne M. Weimann, *The Fair Women* (Chicago: Academy Chicago, 1981), 51.

48. Henry Van Brunt, "Architecture of the World's Columbian Exposition," *Century Magazine* 44 (May 1892): 94. See also Mary N. Woods, "Henry Van Brunt: 'The Historic Styles, Modern Architecture,'" in Craig Zabel and Susan S. Munshower, *American Public Architecture: European Roots and Native Expressions.* Papers in Art History from the Pennsylvania State University, vol. 5 (1989), 83–113

49. Burnham, *The Final Official Report*, part I, vol. 1, p. 71.

50. Burnham and Millet, *The Book of the Builders*, 47.

51. The displays in department stores had also prepared people to see large displays of products. For the relationship between world's fairs and department stores, see Russell Lewis, "Everything under One Roof: World's Fairs and Department Stores in Paris and Chicago," *Chicago History* 13 (Fall 1983), 28–47.

52. Burnham and Millet, *The Book of the Builders*, 47.

53. Van Brunt, "Architecture of the World's Columbian Exposition," 88.

54. Schuyler, "Last Words about the World's Fair," 299.

55. The architectural historian Colin Rowe has also pointed out that the commercial architecture of the Loop and the celebratory architecture of the fair were opposite sides of the same coin. See "Chicago Frame," originally published in *Architectural Review* (1956), and reprinted in Colin Rowe, *The Mathematics of the Ideal Villa and Other Essays* (Cambridge, MA: The MIT Press, 1976), 90–109.

56. Burnham and Millet, *The Book of the Builders*, 29–30.

57. Burnham, "The Organization of the World's Columbian Exposition," 6.

58. Within this biaxial layout, the lagoon and Wooded Island acted as a dividing line between what might be described as the manmade, masculine sphere of the main exposition halls and the natural, feminine sphere of the Woman's Building and Horticulture Building.

59. In the earliest plans the Fine Arts Building was not intended to be placed in Jackson Park, but in the downtown location of Lake Front Park. When, during 1891, it became clear that the entire fair was going to be placed in Jackson Park, the Fine Arts Building could not be placed along the Court of Honor as that was already full. The northern part of the fairgrounds was the only space available.

60. I am grateful to Julia Myers for allowing me to quote from her lecture "Images of Unity and Power in the Court of Honor," which she gave at the College Art Association meeting in Chicago in February 1992.

61. See "Sculpture at the World's Fair," in *The Chicago Record's History of the World's Fair*, 195.

62. *World's Columbian Illustrated* 2 (Dec. 1892), 233.

63. It seems to have been inspired by Renaissance images of winged victories entering a city in a carriage as part of a procession. See Nancy Stieber, "The Triumph of Play: Charts, Carts and Cards," *Art and Design* (Jan.–Feb. 1992): 9–15. The fountain's symbolism was extremely straightforward and unambiguous, as it was meant to convey explicitly the fair's didactic program to the visitors, the majority of whom were not accustomed to reading works of art. In this sense, the sculpture was not so different from Renaissance and Baroque public sculpture, all of which had the function to convey directly the power of the person who had commissioned the work of art.

64. Van Brunt, "Architecture of the World's Columbian Exposition," 94.

65. Stanford White to Frederick MacMonnies, February 25, 1892, Stanford White Correspondence, letter book #5, 161–62. Avery Architectural and Fine Arts Library, Columbia University.

66. Millet called this sculpture the *Spirit of Discovery of the Fifteenth Century* in "The Decoration of the Exposition," *Scribner's Magazine* 12 (Dec. 1892): 702.

67. Burnham, *The Final Official Report*, part II, vol. 4, pp. 16–18.

68. Van Brunt said about this building that it showed how America could adapt its inheritance "of ancient and historic forms to uses never foreshadowed in the civilization of the past." See "The Architectural Event of Our Times," *Engineering Magazine* 6 (Jan. 1894): 439.

69. The placement of these murals in the arcade provided an interesting layer of color on a second level to the "White City." The same happened with the murals in the arcade of the Manufactures and Liberal Arts Building. It is probably because of these murals, in addition to all the flags and pendants, that the fair was called colorful, in spite of its whiteness.

70. Frederick L. Olmsted, "The Landscape Architecture of the World's Columbian Exposition," *The Inland Architect and News Record* 22 (Sept. 1893): 20.

71. Montgomery Schuyler, "State Buildings at the World's Fair," *Architectural Record* 3 (July–Sept. 1893): 55–71.

72. "World's Fair State Buildings," *The Inland Architect and News Record* 19 (Mar. 1892): 25.

FIXING THE IMAGE

Above: *Large plate camera with tripod,*
the type used by professional photographers.

Opposite: *West end of the Grand Basin that*
stood in the center of the White City. Photograph
by C. D. Arnold. Statuary, walkways, water,
bridges, arches, columns, and massive exhibit
halls linked parts of this urban environment.

FIXING THE IMAGE: PHOTOGRAPHY AT THE WORLD'S COLUMBIAN EXPOSITION

by James Gilbert

At the time of the Chicago World's Columbian Exposition in 1893, the technology of photography had entered a phase of rapid and extraordinary development. Camera prices were falling; film had become easier to use; and simpler printing methods were relatively inexpensive. With a large variety of cheap devices on the market, including several models of George Eastman's Kodak snapshot cameras, the number of amateur photographers increased rapidly.[1] At the same time, photography journals multiplied, camera clubs organized, and debates over the aesthetics of camera work preoccupied professional photographers. By every account a festival of visual delights and curiosities, the Chicago fair was a photographer's dream.

For those who directed and financed the fair, photography had the somewhat different, narrower purpose of celebrating a special cultural and aesthetic mission. What architect and chief administrator Daniel Burnham, landscape designer Frederick Law Olmsted, and the Chicago managers of the exposition glorified in the White City was a vision of urban public space, dominated by a neoclassical aesthetic and devoted to the enhancement of city life through a planned and carefully controlled environment. With its integrated visual effects, achieved through painted exteriors, its extensive outdoor art, and its lagoons, bridges, and walkways, the White City represented an idealized world for middle-class urbanites. Exotic and questionable entertainments that represented another and very different urban reality were either excluded, located at the periphery, or placed along the Midway, which ran perpendicular to the White City. The fair managers depended upon this section to generate crucial revenue for the whole enterprise; yet they carefully separated these concessions from the rest of the fair in hopes of convincing the millions of Americans who visited Chicago that the White City should be the model for America's urban future.[2]

Those who planned the fair also sought to control the audience's experience of the exposition. They located buildings carefully; they regulated concessions, performances, and displays; they instructed architects and artists to fulfill their vision

Above: South Water Street market, c. 1893. The bedlam of commerce characterized contemporary Chicago streets. Commerce at the fair, however, especially in the White City, was carefully organized and displayed. Photograph by J. W. Taylor.

Opposite: Dedication ceremonies in front of the courthouse on Adams Street, October 21, 1892. Ceremonies, speeches, parades, and commemorations before and during the fair drew massive but orderly crowds.

of the aesthetically perfect city. Before the fair, the promotion department worked diligently to generate favorable press coverage by carefully controlling the information and images made available to journals, newspapers, and guidebook companies. Photographs depicting the fair were instrumental to this strategy.

But not only could photography shape anticipations, it could also configure memories, fixing a particular visual reality in the minds of those who attended, as well as those who would only glimpse

it through newspaper and journal accounts or through photography souvenir books. Even here, the fair planners hoped to mold the impact of the exposition.[3]

As part of preliminary advertising for the fair, images of the fair created expectations of a visual spectacle. It was difficult, if not impossible, for the prospective tourist to avoid encountering an image of the fair before visiting. Beginning in 1892, views of individual buildings appeared in journals such as *Scientific American* and in leading cultural magazines. Drawn from architectural sketches and plans sent out by the World's Columbian administration, such "designs and cuts" were distributed by the director-general of the fair free of charge to any periodical that would reproduce them. They carried glowing captions recounting the size of the buildings, their display spaces, and anticipated cost.[4]

Throughout 1892 and into the spring of 1893, guidebooks rendered the anticipated fair in etchings, sketches of buildings, and bird's-eye views. Some of these resembled the artistically embellished photographs, called photosketches, that were popular in the souvenir photography books published by Rand McNally during and after the fair. Others, such as *An Accurate and Authentic World's Fair Album*, published by the Unique Parlor Game Company, contained bird's-eye drawings of the fair and sketches of buildings proposed for the White City.[5] Other guidebooks featured elaborate photographs or drawings of the city of Chicago, its monuments, parks, businesses, and residences, and maps and depictions of the principal buildings of the White City.[6] Those visitors who used such guides on the fairgrounds approached buildings and settings that had to some extent already become familiar.

Right: This artistic rendering of the Fisheries Building plan made little effort at verisimilitude. Rather, the artist created a picturesque vision of the exhibit hall seen from an elevated perspective.

Left: A model workingman's house, similar to many contemporary houses in Chicago, was placed on the southern edge of the fairgrounds as part of the New York State exhibit. Unlike the lavishly decorated public buildings, this display was applauded for its frugality and simplicity.

Opposite: Like other bird's-eye views of the fair, this drawing published by Rand McNally of Chicago in 1898 distorted objects in the foreground to provide the illusion of three-dimensionality. The Midway, toward the rear center of the sketch, is scarcely visible.

Right: Part of Arnold's early photographic record of construction, this print, taken April 15, 1892, captured the first arches erected for the Manufactures Building. Arnold centered the arches in his shot, showing them soaring above helter-skelter piles of timber, as if to say: "Here is what is to come." Photograph by C. D. Arnold. Below: Manufactures Building, May 21, 1892. Photograph by C. D. Arnold.

To establish control of images of the fair, the fair administration in 1893 granted the architectural photographer Charles Dudley Arnold and his partner, Harlow D. Higinbotham, son of the president of the Chicago fair board, an exclusive right to commercial photography inside the grounds. Arnold had been hired by the construction department during the building phase of the fair to record progress made on various structures in the White City area. Using large platinum prints, he created a visual record of the construction in a two-volume album that so impressed the architects and the managers that they granted him an exclusive photographic concession, restricting photography by all other professionals and amateurs. Both he and his partner received a salary of two thousand dollars for the months the fair was open, in addition to a commission on all photographs sold.[7] To protect their exclusive contract, the photography

department, which Arnold headed, had permission to call upon the Columbian guards to enforce the strict regulation of who could or could not bring photographic equipment into the fair.

Arnold also had the franchise to sell any photographs made in his studio to guidebooks, journals, and newspapers desiring illustrations of fair buildings and activities. He could grant exceptions to these rules for selected journalists or amateurs if he wished. He also filled orders from journalists and businesses with displays on the grounds. Individuals who did not find a photograph they desired could place a special order. Finally, Arnold was charged with taking photographs of twenty thousand fair employees for their identity badges, although it was reported that "several of the higher officials object to this operation and are refusing to be photographed."[8]

To control a second popular form of photography, the exposition management decided to grant a monopoly to the firm of B. W. Kilburn and James M. Davies, which paid seventeen thousand dollars for exclusive rights to produce stereographic depictions of the fairgrounds. Based upon a simple technology that created what the leading firm of the day, Underwood and Underwood, called "a beautiful illusion, based on scientific truth," stereographic photographs had become immensely popular in the late nineteenth century. Two joined cameras snapped simultaneous shots. When developed, mounted on cardboard or glass, and placed inside a stereographic viewer, these shots appeared highly detailed and three-dimensional.[9] As the *Photographic Times* reported in July 1893, Kilburn was everywhere with his assistants, creating "just the views people want to buy."[10]

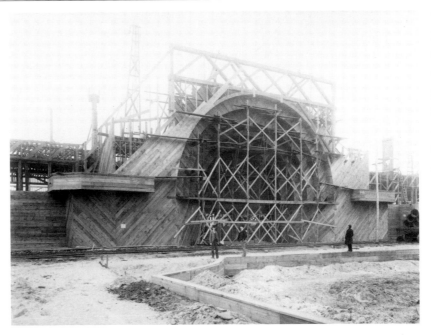

Top: The Transportation Building, designed by Louis Sullivan. This building was one of Arnold's least photographed subjects. Like many other photographers, he focused on the arched doorway, shot from an angle. This was one of the few buildings that Arnold rarely showed in its entirety. Photograph by C. D. Arnold.

This stereograph card produced in 1892 shows part of the archwork during the construction of the Manufactures and Liberal Arts Building. Viewed with a stereograph machine this card gave a vivid, three-dimensional image. The disjunction that made this illusion possible may be seen by comparing the right-hand sides of both prints.

Stereograph cards and viewer.

Despite this favorable notice, people complained about the restrictions set by the administration and attempted to circumvent the rules. Amateurs were forbidden to carry stereoscopic cameras onto the grounds; professionals could do so only by special permission and with payment of a stiff fee. Nonetheless, a few amateurs experimented with holding two cameras side by side that were triggered simultaneously or using one camera for two successive shots with a very slight difference in angle. When the firm of Underwood and Underwood produced stereoscopic images with two cameras and sold them without permission, Kilburn and Davies obtained a permanent injunction against them.[11]

Most onerous to fairgoers was the regulation of amateur photography. If, as estimates suggest, there were one hundred thousand amateurs in the United States at this time, most of them affluent enough to make the trip to the fair, limitations imposed on them severely restricted their ability to take pictures and persuaded many not to bother bringing a camera.[12] For a fee of two dollars a day (four times the price of general admission) a visitor could bring a small, hand-held camera, taking pictures no larger than four by five inches, into the grounds. The Street in Cairo on the Midway charged an additional one dollar for photographic privileges. After signing a release promising not to permit stereoscopic views to be made from any negatives, camera buffs received an identity tag to be attached to the bottom of the camera.

By 1893, advances in practical and cheap camera equipment had greatly reduced the price of taking pictures. A "Daylight Kodak" that could be reloaded outside a darkroom cost about twenty-five dollars for a four-by-five-inch size. This new design meant that amateurs no longer had to own developing equipment or send their cameras back to George Eastman's company in Rochester, New York, for prints and new film, although many still preferred to do so.

The cameras developed by Eastman and other producers in the years immediately before the world's fair were simple and effective. Eastman wrote: "The principle of the Kodak system is the separation of the work that any person whomsoever can do in making a photograph, from the work that only an expert can do."[13] The first Kodak camera, marketed in 1888, contained one hundred exposures and sold for twenty-five dollars, including shoulder strap and leather case. It operated at the push of a button with a key to turn the film. When all of the exposures were used, the camera could be returned to Kodak. For ten dollars, all the shots would be developed and printed, and the camera reloaded and mailed back to the patron.[14]

Amateurs owned a great variety of cameras, including Kodaks and other American models as well as British, German, and French equipment. Other popular models included the new "detective" cameras, which were small devices disguised to resemble watches, hats, or other common objects. These secret gadgets suggested that the candid shot was somehow mysterious or, perhaps, indecent. A large cartoon that appeared in *Puck*

during the summer of 1891 showed leering men at a beach secretly snapping pictures of a woman in a bathing costume.[15]

Most cameras, except the few new models using "daylight" film, still required darkroom reloading; therefore, the amateur was severely limited at the fair by the refusal of the administration to offer facilities for reloading and developing. Many amateurs owned simple, cheap cameras and their own developing and printing equipment, some of which was portable. The problem was partly resolved when several photographic firms provided "darkrooms, with all conveniences for changing plates or films," plus the sale of film and plates at standard prices, in a building inside the grounds near the main entrance.[16] The new South Shore Hotel nearby, which served as the unofficial headquarters for camera buffs, provided more elaborate facilities. As *American Photographer* reported in March

The permit granting one-day's use of a hand-held camera at the fair attempted to appeal to women. It was imprinted on the front with a young girl, primly carrying her Kodak and making a curtsey-like gesture.
Left: Hand-held Kodak "C" camera, c. 1891.

G. Hunter Bartlett of Buffalo, an amateur photographer, captured one of the photographers'—
and tourists'—delights: the illumination of the White City by electric lights during the evening. Facing the Administration Building, the photographer caught the ghostly reflections of the Electricity
Building on the right and Machinery Hall on the left.

1893, the hotel was constructing a darkroom with stalls, sinks, and other conveniences.[17]

Amateurs managed to find other loopholes in the regulations restricting photography at the fair. Some amateurs rented cheap camp chairs for ten cents a day and then rested their cameras on the backs to achieve the stability of a tripod. Some carried small ladders to gain a better perspective. But, as *Wilson's Photographic Magazine* advised: "Pay your fee at the gate; keep the rules and use your eyes before you expose. An attempt to 'circumvent' or steal in any way will doubtless end in arrest and confiscation of apparatus or a fine, for there are plenty of detectives."[18]

For those without their own equipment, cameras could be rented daily from the Kodak Company for two dollars. But no tripods were allowed. The same regulations governed the press, although eventually this code was modified to allow some to use tripods. Amateurs were eventually allowed to pay fifteen dollars for a month's permit to use a four-by-five-inch camera.

These restrictions were aimed not so much at the casual tourist but at the amateur photographer whose equipment might well demand a tripod to steady a large camera with slow film. In addition, the initial lack of darkroom facilities made it difficult and inconvenient to develop film that demanded more complex processes than that of the hand-held Kodak, again a regulation aimed at the skilled amateur.

Regulations at the 1889 Paris Exposition Universelle in Paris had set the precedent for limitations on unofficial photography. At that fair, amateurs and professionals alike paid an entrance fee for their cameras, but no monopoly was

Like many publishers, J. B. Campbell turned to artwork when photographs were inadequate. Here an idealized parade of international visitors pass before Uncle Sam and the symbol of Columbia and pour into the fairgrounds—pictured from a bird's-eye perspective.

The quickest way to get to the fair from downtown Chicago was by train. Passengers could board at the station in Lake Front Park, near the site of the World's Columbian Exposition Auxiliary Congresses. In the background stand the Auditorium Building and the Studebaker Building to its right. Photograph by Copelin Photo.

Photographer C. D. Arnold, above, and his partner, Harlow D. Higinbotham, right.

Opposite: In a style markedly different from his other world's fair photographs, here Arnold photographed only a thin line of buildings from the Wooded Isle, focusing instead on the plants in the foreground. Photograph by C. D. Arnold.

granted to a single firm, and no limit was placed on camera size. Arnold's concession was more extreme and comprehensive, and it resulted in high prices for single photographs. The cost of an eight-by-ten-inch image began at thirty cents. Four-by-five-inch stereoscopic prints from Kilburn and Davies cost twenty cents. For larger Arnold photographs, the price rose to $1.00 for a ten-by-twelve-inch print and $1.50 for a twelve-by-fourteen-inch print. Arnold charged five dollars for a specially commissioned shot, and he retained the copyright even though, as often as not, these were taken by his assistants.[19]

Occasional exceptions were made to these rules. Administrator Harlow N. Higinbotham allowed the Duke of Newcastle to bring his eight-by-ten-inch camera and tripod onto the grounds. Such deviations only increased the anger of amateurs and pro-

fessionals toward the Arnold monopoly. By early summer, the Chicago press was filled with complaints about Arnold's high-handed tactics and about the ungentlemanly behavior of the fair's police. Journals such as the *American Amateur Photographer* (edited by Alfred Stieglitz after July 1893) repeatedly sent letters of protest to the fair administration ways and means committee, asking for a change in the rules. According to the *Chicago Daily Times*, even W. B. Conkey, publisher of the official catalogue of the fair, was denied the right to reproduce photographs because his publication might compete with sales from Arnold's concession. As the *Times* raged, "Arnold and 'Co.', with a patent paternal 'pull' behind the 'Co.' [a reference to Harlow D. Higinbotham] are running the exposition business to suit themselves. They have even arrogated to themselves the right to select their customers."[20] J. B. Campbell, publisher of the *World's Columbian Exposition Illustrated*, also complained bitterly after he had to pay Arnold a steep sum for special photographs whose commercial rights the official photographer retained. Campbell continued to trouble the photography department. According to the *Chicago Evening Post* of June 13, 1893, Campbell was arrested earlier that month for taking photographs on the grounds even though he had a special permit from the director-general of the World's Columbian Exposition commission.[21]

Not only businessmen and journalists protested against Arnold's monopoly. At the World's Fair Auxiliary Congresses held in Chicago and devoted to assessing the state of knowledge and progress, the photography meeting passed a unanimous resolution attacking the photography arrangements made with Arnold:

That it is the sense of this Congress that the burdensome restrictions now placed upon photographers attending the World's Fair Exposition should be removed . . . [and a National Commission established to investigate the Department of Photography and appoint] proper and competent photographers [to take pictures to] do justice to the Exposition.[22]

More than Arnold's monopoly was at stake here. Critics frequently belittled Arnold's pictures. Others reproached the department for the poor quality of commissioned shots done by Arnold's assistants, many of which did not even capture the assigned scene. While there is some truth in these charges, many of Arnold's views are magnificent, even if they demonstrate a stiffly applied aesthetic and repetitive framing devices.

Arnold saw his task, in part, as the recorder of the process of creating the grand fair, and his early construction photographs establish the priority of scale, order, and enterprise visible in the endeavor.[23] The best of his photographs, taken on an eleven-by-fourteen-inch plate with an American Optical Co. camera and printed using the expensive platinum process, have an astounding luminosity and clarity of detail that make them immediately identifiable as his work. The use of photosensitive metal compounds containing silver and platinum had been established during the late nineteenth century. But because of the high price and the special tonal qualities achieved with platinum, this printmaking process quickly became associated with more artistic and professional forms of photography.[24] Arnold's choice of this medium underscored his belief that the photographs he produced had

Opposite: This print illustrates Arnold's emphasis on the monumentality of White City architecture—in this case the Agriculture Building and the Colonnade. The people posed at the bottom suggest the scale of the buildings as well as the scale of the statues. Photograph by C. D. Arnold.

the quality of high art. In their brilliance and almost three-dimensional quality, the photographs underscore the brash and grandiose intentions of the designers of the White City. Arnold's photographs, denuded as they are of crowds, movement, clutter, and distractions, render the White City more perfect than perhaps even the eye could see.

The photographer reiterated several aesthetic principles in his shots. Most of the images were framed, often by a large foreground of water or walkway and sky at the top. Buildings occupied photographs by themselves or as part of ensembles. Rarely did Arnold fragment his vision unless it was to focus on a statue or an entrance, in which case the building itself became the frame. Architectural photographer that he was, he idealized

Arnold raised his camera above the confusion inside the Manufactures and Liberal Arts Building. From this level, the scene is still crowded with people. But by focusing on the tops of the larger display pavilions, Arnold created the illusion of a city skyline seen from a bird's-eye view. Photograph by C. D. Arnold.

Right: This photograph from Portrait Types of the Midway *establishes the identity and culture of these Turkish men through dress, a hookah, or communal pipe, and swords. Photograph by J. J. Gibson.*

Below right: Arnold's photographs of people show them in stereotypical roles. He preferred his subjects to appear as a uniform group rather than as individuals, as in this photograph of young girls he fashioned as housekeepers. Photograph by C. D. Arnold.

Opposite: Unlike Arnold's typical group photographs of people, these gentlemen of the fair administration require no tools or distinctive costumes. They have struck informal poses, appearing more as individuals than as a group. Photograph by C. D. Arnold.

buildings in compositions that reduced the surroundings to the role of a setting.

Because crowds might confuse the viewer, distract the eye, and divert attention from the monumentality of buildings, Arnold rarely focused on large numbers of fair visitors in his shots. Most include a few individuals, perhaps to emphasize the size of the subject, but buildings, not people, were clearly the center of attention. Arnold carefully used light and camera angles to capture the most impressive features of buildings.

Perspective also played a major role in his choice of angles and ensembles. He took photographs from on top of other buildings, looking down on the White City, producing views reminiscent of the bird's-eye etchings so popular in guidebooks and souvenir books. He applied the same technique to several dramatic interior shots. Other views incorporated nature as a framing device: he used lagoons and waterways to push the photographed building off into the distance and then draw it back through its reflection in the water. Such techniques lent a sense of quiet and decorum, an aesthetic order to what in reality were bustling thoroughfares and crowded exhibits, made so by the disorderly meandering of huge crowds of visitors.

One of Arnold's favorite photographic subjects was outdoor art work, particularly statues of human figures or animals. Like buildings, he placed these at the center of his shots and tried to capture them in their entirety, or he used them as a reference point, a guide to the eye for viewing a building. When photographing live subjects, he used much the same technique. People appear in his photographs as framing devices or suggestions of size and shape. In part limited by the photographic

The interior of the Woman's Building, viewed from the balcony, presented William H. Jackson with the challenge of an indoor shot and a long perspective. The result was a splendid photograph with three-dimensional monumentality. Photograph by W. H. Jackson.

The marvels of the fair included the Krupp Gun Exhibit. This image of the interior was a favorite of visitors, souvenir books, and photographers.

technology and the slow film, Arnold's close-up portrait studies are sometimes rigidly posed. The popular tradition in painting throughout the nineteenth century of "portrait types," in which figures were positioned in an idealized setting that suggested something of their work or social position, had also been adopted by photographers.[25]

Arnold used this format when he photographed "Midway Types"[26] astride horses or camels, holding swords or agricultural implements, wearing traditional garb, and posed in front of the exhibits where they worked. These figures were meant to represent the cultures on display on the Midway: Egyptians, Algerians, Turks, Dahomeyans, Germans, and Irish. He avoided spontaneous gestures; he looked over no shoulders, nor did he seem to wish to catch his subjects unaware. He presented the exotic peoples of the Midway as benign objects to be viewed and studied. He suggested nothing about their perspective, nor was he interested in capturing the interaction between tourists and the peoples on display. Arnold generally avoided candid shots of everyday visitors to the fair. His interests lay in the monumental, permanent qualities of the White City, contrasted with the peculiarities of the Midway. The result was a very identifiable, if formal, version of the fair, reproduced in photographs of high quality.

Arnold's autocratic control over public photography finally alienated so many important people that it raised doubts in the minds of the fair administrators and even in his benefactor, Harlow N. Higinbotham. The national commission of the World's Columbian Exposition had over the summer urged curbing Arnold's power. The Chicago press vigorously criticized the photographer, and some journals even suggested replacing Arnold with the famous landscape photographer William Henry Jackson.[27] When, in the fall of 1893, Arnold refused to produce a final set of official negatives, Daniel Burnham commissioned Jackson to produce one hundred eleven-by-fourteen-inch negatives for the official history. The new photographer was paid one thousand dollars for his efforts. His prints were not, however, published in the final history, perhaps, as historian Peter Hales contends, because they had a somewhat less celebratory quality to them.[28]

Jackson's photographs did appear in two versions, *The White City as it Is* and *Jackson's Famous Pictures of the World's Fair*, and here we can see what might have distressed the fair's management. Taken after the fair had closed, Jackson's views include workmen, wagons, and clean-up crews. They are also less monumental and less controlled than Arnold's versions. But many of Jackson's perspectives are surprisingly similar, and some of the monumentality of Arnold remains.[29] While Jackson's photographic books may have eventually been more popular, Arnold still had a decisive impact on defining the photographic vision of the fair. He accomplished this because of his control of the photography, and because the prints he produced gave visual embodiment to the aesthetic purposes of those who designed the fair.

Despite the objections to stringent rules and an undercurrent of criticism of Arnold's vision, there is considerable evidence that the monumental and picturesque were also principles of the amateur aesthetic code. F. Dundas Todd, a leading amateur and publisher of the book, *World's Fair through a Camera: Snap Shots by an Artist*, wrote an early camera guide to the fair that appeared in the April edition of *American Amateur Photographer*. Identifying spots

The Columbian Guards performed as an internal police force for the fair. One of their duties was to enforce restrictions on photography. Souvenir books stressed the order maintained on the grounds in spite of huge crowds. Photograph by J. J. Gibson.

from which to capture the most picturesque views, Todd warned against "the ground south of the Agricultural Hall, or in the Midway Plaisance, as these are in so chaotic a condition that it is difficult to

form any estimates of their possibilities."[30] When he collected his own photographs for publication somewhat later, many of them resembled Arnold's work, concentrating on the same monumental views. His shots of Midway individuals were as posed and stiff as Arnold's portraits. Few if any candid shots of individuals or crowds existed. The accidental was excluded.[31]

More elaborate advice on photographic perspectives for amateurs came from Chicago novelist Henry B. Fuller in *Chicago Record's History of the World's Fair*. This long piece explained the photographic rules at the fairgrounds, listed the fees, and defined proper camera etiquette. His recommendations were aimed at the amateur searching for the picturesque. Of the "Kodak Fiend, pure and simple, freaking his way through the plaisance, I shall have nothing to say," he began. Beyond warning of the problems in photographing smoke coming from the *Whaleback* (the ship that connected the fairgrounds to downtown), Fuller cautioned against including anything "left behind by slovenly lunchers" or unsightly "broken-backed benches." Another peril was the Midway. Here the photographer would find it difficult to capture his subjects "harmoniously reinforced by proper backgrounds and accessories." Unsightly juxtapositions, such as advertisements for Milwaukee Beer in front of a mosque or signs in the Turkish village that render it "no more inviting than an equal frontage taken out of a certain part of State Street," obscured the picturesque.

Curiously, Fuller's advice can be read as an unintentional advertisement for Arnold's souvenir photographs. Arnold had successfully captured exactly those scenes that Fuller worried might be too difficult for the amateur to reproduce. The official pho-

Left: An ever-present problem for the photographer, whether amateur or professional, was the curious bystander who wanted to intrude into the picture. Here the photographer of the Swedish building had focused his distant shot to capture the building; the people in front of it were an indistinguishable crowd. The boy leaning into view ruined this composition.

Above: Arnold enjoyed taking pictures of his crew at work. Here the official photographers pose with their camera and tripod and another "Midway type." Photograph by C. D. Arnold.

Opposite: This scene of lunchtime on the Grand Basin near the Peristyle of the White City was not what image-makers of the fair wished to publicize.

This shot of the MacMonnies Fountain *(foreground),* Grand Basin, *and* Statue of the Republic *demonstrates the serendipity of timing. The* Whaleback *steamer had just left its dock and, as evidenced by the thick smoke, was plowing toward Chicago.*

tographer had avoided introducing distracting and disorderly objects or the perspectives that Fuller warned created hazards for the amateur. In assessing amateur efforts to photograph the Midway, *Cosmopolitan* underscored the same predicament for the amateur: "The scene was all too comprehensive for him to grasp it in its entirety; there was no beginning or ending with anything like definition."[32]

Given the limitations on photography and the availability of excellent prints for sale, it is not surprising that the numbers of amateur photographers on the fairgrounds were low. In a July interview, Arnold disclosed that fifty to sixty photographic permits were issued during the average week, with one hundred permits at the highest point.[33] (These figures suggest around two thousand amateur permits sold during the duration of the fair.) Technology and the rules favored the simplest, most practical photographic equipment. The *Photographic Times* suggested in early 1893 that "the 'Kodak fiend' will have a decided advantage over the 'fiend' with a glass-plate camera, or even over the one using cut films." Because initially no darkroom facilities were available on the grounds, "the Kodaker with his roll of film weighing but a few ounces will be able to make 100 exposures for his new investment of $2."[34]

Still, camera companies did their best to remind travelers to the fair of its photographic possibilities. Signs painted on barns along the railway from New York to Chicago encouraged travelers to "Take a Kodak with You" or to purchase Blair's cameras. Many of these advertisements were directed at women. *Munsey's* magazine reported that hundreds of camera clubs existed throughout the United States in 1894 with a "great army of snap

Crowds and clutter were inevitable in any shot of the Midway, even for Arnold. Unlike the White City, the Midway bustled with commerce and consumption. Photograph by C. D. Arnold.

Taken from Laird and Lee's Glimpses of the World's Fair, *this print catches the "Kodak Fiend" in action. Numerous women in the 1890s owned and operated cameras. Since many Americans did not yet consider photography as an ordinary tourist activity, photographers' activities could be disruptive.*

This photograph of the Ferris Wheel on the Midway, shot from the grounds of the new University of Chicago, suggests the difficulties of using a hand-held camera.

shot enthusiasts." A "great many women take pictures nowadays," the article continued. Some, such as Mrs. N. Gray Bartlett, had her work on view in the Woman's Building and the Illinois State Building at the fair.[35]

The popular term "Kodak fiend" suggested serious questions about the etiquette of public photography that relate, in part, to the large number of women among amateurs. In 1900, for example, the *Ladies' Home Journal* ran an editorial describing

"Kodak manners." Sometimes, it warned, the camera owner departed from "all good breeding." Etiquette had not kept pace with technology. "It is a difficult point for some people to understand that there are those who have a strong prejudice against being promiscuously 'snapped at' through a camera. Girls and young women otherwise well behaved are particularly heedless of the feeling of others on this point."[36] While male amateurs could be dismissed for the same sort of intrusiveness, propriety particularly affected women amateurs. The Kodak Company seemed well aware of this possible limitation when it depicted the ideal "Kodak Girl" for *Photographic Times* in 1893 as an amateur who carried her small camera, loaded with one hundred exposures: "She is sensible as well as good looking."[37] Women also suffered from traditional restraints on their public activities. This was just one further obstacle to their participation in amateur photography at the fair.[38]

Nonetheless amateur photography provided an important record of landscape and architecture, of "Midway types," of exotic settings seen by Americans who attended the fair and by thousands who did not. *Cosmopolitan*, in late 1893, estimated that thousands became camera enthusiasts because of the fair. As photography became more common, individuals grew accustomed to camera carriers, and the development of a public photographic etiquette further popularized the apparatus. The *Chicago Evening Post* assured its readers that amateurs were the most "amiable of modern cranks. He or she (just as often as not it is she) does no manner of harm to any living creature, but on the contrary does a good deal of good, besides having a barrel of fun."[39]

Photographs for sale included those of glamorous women such as May Morrell of the Congress of Beauties on the Midway. This image, mounted on stiff cardboard, was sold as part of a series of "Gibson cards" by J. J. Gibson of Chicago.

A bird's-eye view gives a good sense of the fair ensemble in its urban setting. With the Wooded Isle in the foreground, the camera focuses on the Woman's Building to the right. In the distance is the Midway, the Ferris Wheel, the University of Chicago on the right and beyond it, and surrounding the sides of the park, the hotel area where many tourists stayed.

The *American Annual of Photography and Photographic Times* was equally enthusiastic when it wrote in 1894, "A photographic record of a pleasure jaunt, a business trip, or a vacation tour, is the best record a man can keep, and is the most charming form of diary to read and re-read over and over again."[40] In this fashion, *Cosmopolitan* estimated, many "sets of pictures of the White City will journey through the States, the British Isles, across the Continent, China, India, Japan, Australia, and back again to the States."[41] If this last estimate of the worldwide interest is somewhat overenthusiastic, it reveals the existence of multiple audiences for world's fair snapshots.

Camera clubs across the nation exchanged or exhibited world's fair photography. The American Lantern-Slide Interchange sponsored by camera clubs exchanged photographs, held exhibitions, and awarded prizes. With such multiple viewings, amateur photography reached a much wider audience than the friends or relatives of the average "camera fiend."

Still, it was probably Arnold's vision that most deeply shaped the photographic record of the fair. Many individual prints were sold to fair visitors. His photographs appeared widely in journals, newspapers, and souvenir photography books. Two of these souvenir collections illustrate Arnold's aesthetic: *The Great White City: A Picture Gallery of the World's Fair and Midway Plaisance*, a large scale, ten-volume edition containing sixteen photographs each, released by W. B. Conkey Company, and *Beautiful Scenes of the White City*, published in New York. *Scenes* even described the photographic process as a daring aesthetic feat: "The artist has planted the tripod upon the roof of the Peristyle and has

This unusual candid shot captures a visitor's shocked reaction as the half-naked Samoan Villagers parade by —not the ordinary, stolid, and posed shot of "Midway types."

The Eastman Kodak booth whetted the public's appetite for the latest in photographic technology.

Opposite: The Administration Building from the Wooded Isle Bridge.

After the fair closed and devastating fires swept through it, even its ruins were reimagined by photography. The Peristyle burned on January 8, 1894, right. Through the twisted metal and charred struts, the Statue of the Republic and surviving buildings appeared as mystical memories of grandeur, opposite.

Photographers sometimes caught people off-guard, as in this photograph of sleepimg chair pushers. These chairs, available for tourists, were among the curiosities at the fair.

pointed his reproductive camera slightly southwest, and a magnificent view has been the result."[42] In addition, Arnold and Higinbotham's own *Official Views* contained some of Arnold's most exemplary work. It opened with several shimmering photographs of the White City and the Court of Honor, then moved to several interiors and foreign government buildings. The last section included

curiosities such as the rolling chairs for tourists and carefully posed "Midway types." The final photograph returned to the Court of Honor, as if to instruct the viewer that this was where imagination and memory should begin and end.[43]

Still, differences in vision developed. Those souvenir books that did not feature Arnold prints, such as Henry E. Flower's *Glimpses of the World's Fair*, were

distinctly less stately. Buildings were sometimes truncated or set to one side. There were frequent, inconsequential views, shot over the backs of fair visitors. Several photographs had sketched-in cloud formations, giving them a fake appearance. Another common sort of souvenir book was A. Wittemann's *Chicago and the World's Columbian Exposition*. This book included shots of crowded Chicago streets, huge buildings, monuments, and parks in addition to conventional photographs of the fair.[44]

But even when Arnold's actual work was not reproduced, shots by other professionals tended to replicate his perspectives and interests. The wide distribution of his work had some influence. No doubt the prevailing aesthetic of photography that stressed the picturesque, the idealized landscape, the portrait, and the framed and centered shot—while deemphasizing the ordinary and candid—also accounted for some of the resemblance.

To the present-day observer looking back on this period of photographic history and the record left in books and libraries, the tendency is to believe that Arnold's is the only perspective and that he and the fair administration successfully shaped how visitors saw and remembered the fair and how the rest of the public imagined it. To a degree this is true. An important undercurrent of amateur work successfully challenged Arnold's monopoly and provided a somewhat different perspective on the fair. But this visual chronicle has for the most part vanished from the public record. And so we are left with a view of the fair that reproduces the vision that was intended by those who planned the exposition: a monumental White City and a carefully controlled and exotic Midway.

NOTES

I wish to thank Connie Casey for her enormous help in identifying and selecting photographs for this essay.

1. Sarah Greenough, "The Economic Incentives, Social Inducements, and Aesthetic Issues of American Pictorial Photography, 1880–1892," in *Photography in Nineteenth-Century America*, ed. Martha A. Sandweis(Fort Worth: Amon Carter Museum, 1991), 259–61. In this essay, I will use amateur to apply to those photographers who used cameras as part of an elaborate hobby or interest. They should be differentiated from casual users of cameras who had little knowledge of the technology of developing and print-making.

2. Neil Harris, *Cultural Excursions: Marketing Appetites and Cultural Tastes in Modern America* (Chicago: University of Chicago Press, 1990) .

3. Photography was an important element of display at the fair. Major photographic companies such as Eastman Kodak, Blair, and Bausch and Lomb Opticals had exhibits at the fair. Inside the fairgrounds, as the *Photographic Times* reported, almost every exhibit contained "photographs of the things exhibited as well as the objects themselves, and many are the photographs of entire exhibits to be seen in the various buildings." This interplay between photograph and exhibit underscored the importance of the photograph for commercial artistic purposes. Despite this widespread use of photographs to record and mirror what was actually seen, the exposition administration devoted only a passing glance at photography as an art. There were photographic exhibits in the Liberal Arts Building and also in the United States pavilion. W. H. Jackson had a noteworthy exhibit of landscapes and of Washington, D.C. And there was also the largest photograph in the world, assembled from seven negatives taken at the Philadelphia Centennial several years before.

   In the small gallery of the Liberal Arts Building only fifty or so professionals were chosen to exhibit their works. Six women were chosen by the administration to exhibit, but all their entries were sent to the Woman's Building. Few amateur photographers were chosen, and no prizes were awarded for any entries. See *Photographic Times* 23 (July 28, 1893): 401 and "The Photographic Display at the World's Fair," *American Amateur Photographer* 5 (Feb. 1893): 74.

4. "The World's Fair Official Photographer and His Monopolistic Concession," *American Amateur Photographer* 5 (May 1893): 218.

5. *An Accurate and Authentic World's Fair Album* (Chicago: Unique Parlor Game Co., 1892). See also *Columbian Exposition and Chicago's Wonders* (Chicago: Exposition Guide Co., 1893). This slight, mini-guidebook contained color lithographs of proposed buildings and long paeans to their size and cost.

6. See, for example, *Handy Guide to Chicago and the World's Columbian Exposition* (Chicago: Rand McNally & Co., 1893).

7. Greenough, "Economic Incentives," 318.

8. *American Amateur Photographer* 5 (May 1893): 216. This may appear to be an onerous task, but Arnold's staff did the work, and the process undoubtedly earned him considerable prestige. It also reinforced the importance of photography at the fair.

9. Underwood and Underwood, *A Trip Around the World Representing Life, Customs, and Scenes of Different Countries, Arranged in the Form of a Tour in which You, Your Family, and Your Friends Can Join* (New York: Underwood and Underwood, 1895), n.p. In a 1904 book, *The United States through a Stereoscope*, Underwood and Underwood spoke of its photographs in very much the same language that guidebooks depicted the Chicago world's fair: as a guided tour through the wonders of the world. (New York: Underwood and Underwood, 1904).

10. *Photographic Times* 23 (July 28, 1893): 400.

11. *American Amateur Photographer* 5 (Aug. 1893): 417.

12. *Chicago Evening Post*, May 17, 1893. Amateurs learned their art from photographic journals, camera clubs, and from professional teachers such as the Chautauqua Association, which offered correspondence classes on basic techniques of photography and development and printing.

13. *American Amateur Photographer*. See several stories in the July 1893 issue, pp. 319, 320, 322.

14. *Chicago Daily Times*, Apr. 14, 1893.

15. *American Amateur Photographer* 5 (May 1893): 218. The exposition commission represented the national organization of the world's fair, not the local administration of Burnham and others who set policy.

16. "Photography at the World's Fair," *American Amateur Photographer* 5 (Aug. 1893): 369.

17. See Peter Hales, *Silver Cities: The Photography of American Urbanization, 1839–1915* (Philadelphia: Temple University Press, 1984). Hales is particularly astute in discussing Arnold's aesthetic ideals and the contrast (slight but significant) between his work and that of William Henry Jackson.

18. James Reilly, *Care and Identification of 19th Century Photographic Prints* (Rochester: Eastman Kodak Co., 1986), 8. See also John F. Maloney, *Vintage Cameras and Images* (Florence, AL: Books Americana, 1981), 313.

19. Alan Trachtenberg, *Reading American Photographs: Images as History, Mathew Brady to Walker Evans* (New York: Hill and Wang, 1989), 54.

20. This derogatory term was widely used to describe representatives of displays on the Midway. It fit the evolutionary scheme originally designed for the Midway, to illustrate the progress of civilization from its humble representatives in Africa and the Far East to its highest achievements in the United States. See Robert W. Rydell, *All the World's a Fair: Visions of Empire at American International Expositions, 1876–1916* (Chicago: University of Chicago Press, 1984).

21. Letter from J. F. Ryder, Aug. 9, 1893 to *Wilson's Photographic Magazine* 30 (Sept. 1893), makes this suggestion.

22. Peter Hales, *William Henry Jackson and the Transformation of the American Landscape* (Philadelphia: Temple University Press, 1988), 202–203.

23. Ibid., 207–209. Hales indicates that Jackson's books swept the market after the fair and helped crowd out Arnold's pictures. See William Henry Jackson, *The White City* (*As it Was*) (Chicago: H. Tammen, 1894) and William Henry Jackson, *Jackson's Famous Pictures* (Chicago: White City Art Company, 1894).

24. Brian Coe, *Cameras: From Daguerreotype to Instant Pictures* (Gothenburg: Crown Publishers, 1978), 83.

25. Maloney, *Vintage Cameras*, 11–12.

26. William Welling, *Photography in America: The Formative Years, 1839–1900* (New York: Crowell, 1978), 334.

27. W. H. Walmsley, "Photographing at the Columbian Fair," *Photographic Times* 23 (Dec. 1893): 688.

28. "World's Fair Photographic Privilege," *American Amateur Photographer* 5 (March 1893): 121.

29. "Photography at the World's Fair—How to Manage It," *Wilson's Photographic Magazine* 30 (Apr. 1893): 158, 160.

30. Frederick Dundas Todd, *American Amateur Photographer*, 5 (April 1893): 166ff.

31. Frederick Dundas Todd et al., *World's Fair Through a Camera: Snap Shots by an Artist* (St. Louis: Woodward and Tiernan, 1893), passim.

32. Henry B. Fuller, "Amateur Photography at the Fair," in Henry Fuller et al., *Chicago Record's History of the World's Fair* (Chicago: Chicago Daily News Co., 1893), 107-26. See also Horace Markley, "Amateur Photography at the World's Fair," *Cosmopolitan* 16 (Dec. 1893): 166.

33. "Interview with C. D. Arnold," *Photographic Times* 23 (Aug. 4, 1893): 417.

34. *Photographic Times* 23 (Jan. 6, 1893): 8. Richard Hines, Jr., in 1898, explained that there was "no more suitable work for women than photography, whether she takes it up with a view of making it a profession, or simply as a delightful pastime to give pleasure to herself and others." Women, he concluded, were particularly suited, physically and temperamentally, for the work. Quoted in Peter E. Palmquist, ed., *Camera Fiends and Kodak Girls* (New York: Midmarch Arts Press, 1989), 77.

35. Frank W. Crane, "American Woman Photographers," *Munsey's Magazine* 11 (July 1894): 398–405.

36. *Photographic Times* 23 (Mar. 24, 1893): 157.

37. "Kodak Manners," *Ladies Home Journal* 17 (Feb. 1900): 16. The term "snapshot" stems, apparently, from an older English usage describing a hurried shotgun blast at game.

38. C. Jane Gover, *The Positive Image: Women Photographers in Turn of the Century America* (Albany: State University of New York Press, 1988), passim. Catherine Weed Barnes, a well-known amateur, obviously resented restrictions and dismissal of women photographers. In an 1891 article she wrote: "Humor is one thing, but broad, vulgar farce emphatically, another, and most of the so-called 'funny' articles on camera work and workers can safely be classified under the latter head." In "The Real and the Ideal," *American Amateur Photographer* 3 (Feb. 1891): 59.

39. *Chicago Evening Post*, May 12, 1893.

40. Edward Manser, "Take a Camera with You," *American Annual of Photography and Photographic Times Almanac for* 1894 (New York: Scoville & Adams, 1894): 167.

41. Markley, "Amateur Photography," 168, 170.

42. *The Great White City: A Picture Gallery of the World's Fair and Midway Plaisance*, 10 parts (Chicago: A. Swan Brown, 1894); and William H. Lee, *Beautiful Scenes of the White City*, Farewell Edition (New York: George Crain, 1894).

43. C. D. Arnold and H. D. Higinbotham, *Official Views of the World's Columbian Exposition* (Chicago: Chicago Photo-Gravure Co., 1893).

44. Henry E. Flower, *Glimpses of the World's Fair* (Philadelphia: Henry E. Flower, 1893) and A. Wittemann, *Chicago and the World's Columbian Exposition* (Chicago: A. Wittemann, 1893).

In this lithograph Columbia presents the World's Columbian Exposition as the high point of civilization and the ultimate product of Columbus's voyage to the Americas. Lithograph by Rodolfo Morgari.

Left: This lithograph advertised the Chicago Day celebration at the fair, October 9, 1893, which commemorated the anniversary of the Great Chicago Fire of 1871. Above and right: A pop-up souvenir book from the World's Columbian Exposition.

This souvenir fan featured
a bird's-eye view of the fair.

The attractions of the Midway inspired popular music, such as the "Cairo Street Waltz," dedicated to the managers of Cairo Street.

PUCK'S SUGGESTION FOR THE WORLD'S FAIR —— THE "COLOSSUS OF CHICAGO" WOULD KNOCK OUT THE EIFFEL TOWER.

Left: This cartoon from World's Fair Puck *poked fun at the attempts by fair organizers to create a structure that would symbolize the exposition and outdo the Eiffel Tower. The Midway's Ferris Wheel became the most popular representation of the fair, appearing on numerous souvenirs and inspiring musical compositions, above.*

Hand-tinted photographs of the Irish village and Blarney Castle, top, and the Street in Cairo, bottom. Right: Cover illustration from The Inter-Ocean, October 9, 1893.

A souvenir map of the World's Columbian Exposition.

Scene from the Streets
of Cairo, *watercolor by
Thur De Thulstrup.*

A CULTURAL FRANKENSTEIN?

A Cultural Frankenstein?
The Chicago World's
Columbian Exposition
of 1893

by Robert W. Rydell

Thirty years after more than a half-million Americans died in a bloody civil war, five years after a terrorist threw a bomb in Chicago's Haymarket Square, one year before massive strikes in Pullman's company town outside of the city, and three short years after the U.S. Army's assault on Native Americans at Wounded Knee, South Dakota, the Chicago World's Columbian Exposition opened to commemorate the four-hundredth anniversary of Columbus's arrival in the New World. As contemporaries noted and recent scholarship has confirmed, the fair was a landmark event in American history. Its neoclassical White City reshaped the public architecture of the nation; its World's Congresses gathered intellectuals, labor leaders, and social reformers to debate significant political and philosophical issues of the age; and its Midway Plaisance bestowed the stamp of legitimacy on mass entertainment as a vital component of American culture.[1]

While the fair influenced American life in fundamental ways, it did not give all Americans equal cause for celebration. African-Americans and Native Americans were denied the opportunity to partici-pate on equal terms with whites, while women were refused the opportunity to participate on equal terms with men. Precisely because they saw the fair for what it was—a powerful instrument for reaffirming existing attitudes regarding race and gender—Americans in positions of relative powerlessness debated the fair among themselves and adopted various strategies of accommodation and resistance to meet the challenge of the future as projected at the exposition.

These concerns about representation were not limited to Americans. To reinforce exposition promoters' visions of America's national progress and ambitions to compete with European powers for an overseas empire, the Chicago fair, like contemporary European world's fairs, also featured displays of people from Africa, Asia, the Dutch East Indies, and the Middle East. Read from the vantage point of people typed as "exotic" or "savage" and displayed, for the most part, as living ethnological exhibits along the Midway or ghettoized in the fair's Anthropology Department, the exposition stood as an artifact—an ideological construct—of the age of Western imperialism. The fair posed

*On August 25, 1893, Fred-
erick Douglass, U.S. minister to Haiti, delivered an
impassioned speech at the
fair entitled "The Race Problem in America."*

many questions about who would be included—
and on what terms—in the march of civilization
towards the utopia forecast by the fair's promoters. From the perspective of nonwhites represented at the fair, especially in light of the smallpox
epidemic precipitated by the exposition, the
Chicago fair seemed less like a dream city than a
nightmare come true.

As soon as plans for the Chicago fair were
announced in 1890, African-Americans began
planning for their participation in the hope that
Chicago's exposition authorities would agree to
exhibits that would highlight African-American
achievements since emancipation. But, on the
basis of their experience with America's earlier
international expositions, there were not many
reasons for optimism. The 1876 Philadelphia Centennial Exhibition had generally excluded African-
American exhibits, and police had prevented
former slave and abolitionist Frederick Douglass
from sitting on the platform with opening-day
speakers. At the 1884–85 New Orleans World's
Industrial and Cotton Exposition, the situation was
not much better. Even with the help of the federal
government, African-Americans succeeded only
in establishing a small exhibit devoted to advances
in industrial education since emancipation. Clearly,
since the decision-making power at the World's
Columbian Exposition remained in the hands of
whites, creating African-American exhibits at the
Chicago fair would require a struggle.[2]

That African-Americans had reason to be con-
cerned became apparent when the exposition's
directors decided that all proposed exhibits for
state buildings would have to be approved by com-
mittees made up of whites. This decision effectively

meant that most of the exhibits that African-Americans had been organizing through their own network of county and state fairs would be excluded from the World's Columbian Exposition, especially from buildings organized to represent southern states. When the exposition's Board of Lady Managers, the administrative unit responsible for selecting exhibits for the Woman's Building, refused to allow a black woman to serve as a member, the black press exploded with rage. "We object," the *New York Age* declared. "We carry our objection so far that if the matter was left to our determination we would advise the race to have nothing whatever to do with the Columbian Exposition or the management of it." The situation was only marginally better with the national commission created by Congress to oversee the organization of the fair. After a year of bitter disappointment, African-Americans scored a minor victory when Hale G. Parker, a black school principal from St. Louis, was finally appointed as an alternate commissioner. But this appointment smacked of tokenism and did nothing to mollify the growing concern among African-Americans that their contributions to building the American republic would be ignored, if not ridiculed, at the fair.[3]

How should African-Americans respond to the overt racism manifested by exposition authorities? This question became particularly acute when world's fair organizers yielded to the demands by some black musicians, artists, and writers, including violinist Will Marion Cook and poet Paul Lawrence Dunbar, that there be a special day at the fair that would, in their opinion, resemble special days set aside at the fair to honor white ethnic groups. Variously called Jubilee or Colored People's Day, this event sharply divided African-Americans.

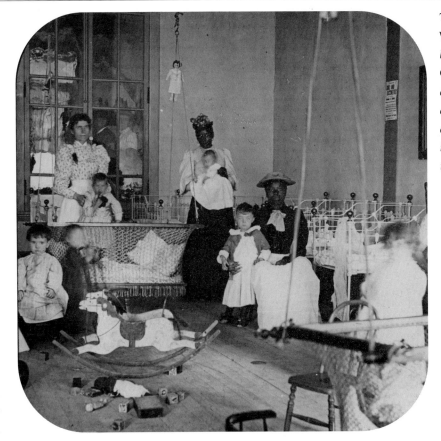

The New York Board of Women Managers established the nursery in the Children's Building to exhibit advanced day care methods. Parents could leave their children in the care of nurses while they enjoyed the fair.

Some, led by Ida B. Wells, the famous antilynching crusader and editor of the *Memphis Free Speech*, urged African-Americans to boycott the fair. Others, led by Frederick Douglass, who served as Haiti's representative at the fair, saw in the occasion an opportunity to condemn white supremacy and to showcase black accomplishments.[4]

The debate between Wells and Douglass struck nerves already rubbed raw by months of frustration about the fair. The nation's most widely circulated black newspaper, the *Indianapolis Freeman*, railed against Jubilee Day: "The Board of Directors have

Midway villages reinforced
suppositions about the supe-
riority of Euro-American
culture. Right: Visitors were
asked to note the Dahome-
yans' "regretful absence of
tailor-made clothes."

Opposite: A cartoon from
World's Fair Puck poked
fun at the clothing of other
cultures.

furnished the day, some members of the race have pledged to furnish the 'niggers,' (in our presence Negroes), and if some thoughtful and philanthropic white man is willing to furnish watermelons, why should he be gibbeted?"[5]

On August 25, the day set aside for Colored People's Day, Douglass arrived at the fairgrounds only to find that watermelon stands had been set up in an effort to trivialize the occasion. For an instant, it appeared that Douglass's critics had been right.

But Douglass was determined to proceed with the speech he had planned to deliver, "The Race Problem in America," despite the catcalls of white hecklers. As Paul Dunbar later recalled, Douglass sounded like the abolitionist orator of old. "Men talk of the Negro problem," Douglass intoned. "There is no Negro problem. The problem is whether the American people have loyalty enough, honor enough, patriotism enough, to live up to their own Constitution." Barely pausing for breath,

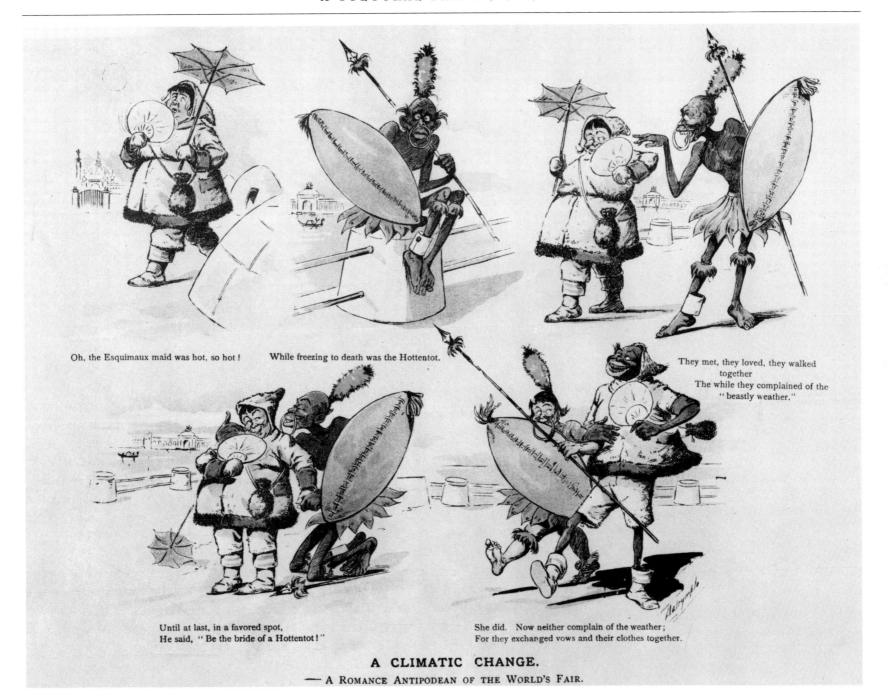

Oh, the Esquimaux maid was hot, so hot !   While freezing to death was the Hottentot.

They met, they loved, they walked together
The while they complained of the "beastly weather."

Until at last, in a favored spot,
He said, " Be the bride of a Hottentot ! "

She did. Now neither complain of the weather ;
For they exchanged vows and their clothes together.

A CLIMATIC CHANGE.
— A ROMANCE ANTIPODEAN OF THE WORLD'S FAIR.

Ida B. Wells raised the money for printing The Reason Why. The Colored American is not in the Columbian Exposition, *which criticized the exclusion of African-Americans from the fair, by helping Chicago's black women to organize fund-raising meetings.*

Douglass added: "We fought for your country, we ask that we be treated as well as those who fought against your country. We love your country. We ask that you treat us as well as you do those who only love a part of it."[6]

The audience was small, but at least one person, Ida Wells, was deeply impressed by Douglass's impassioned remarks. She apologized to Douglass for having questioned the wisdom of participating in the fair and declared that his speech "had done more to bring our cause to the attention of the American people than anything else which had happened during the fair."[7]

Wells and Douglass did more than mend fences. They agreed to collaborate with Chicago newspaper editor Ferdinand L. Barnett, Wells's future husband, and several other prominent African-Americans. Together they issued a pamphlet entitled *The Reason Why. The Colored American is not in the* World's Columbian *Exposition*. This pamphlet remains a noteworthy, if largely forgotten, historical document. The authors detailed the horrors confronting African-Americans in post-Reconstruction America and sharply criticized the moral turpitude of Chicago's world's fair organizers. Douglass wrote the introduction, addressing it to "the good opinion of the world." The absence of exhibits by African-Americans, Douglass emphasized, was not due to "indifference and indolence" on the part of former slaves and their children, but to the hypocrisy of exposition organizers whose values stood "in flagrant contradiction to boasted American Republican liberty and civilization." "There are many good things concerning our country and countrymen of which we would be glad to tell in this pamphlet, if we could do so," Douglass insisted.:

We would like for instance to tell our visitors that the moral progress of the American people has kept even pace with their enterprise and their material civilization; that practices by the ruling class has gone on hand in hand with American professions, that two hundred and sixty years of progress and enlightenment have banished barbarism and hate from the United States; . . . that American liberty is now the undisputed possession of all the American people; that American law is now the shield alike of black and white; that the spirit of slavery and class domination has no longer any lurking place in any part of this country; . . . that here Negroes are not tortured, shot, hanged or burned to death, merely on suspicion of crime and without ever seeing a judge, a jury or advocate; . . . and that the World's Fair now in progress, is not a whited sepulcher.

"But," Douglass concluded, "nothing of all this can be said, without qualification and without flagrant disregard of the truth."[8]

In their contribution to *The Reason Why*, Wells and Barnett called attention to the social and legal conditions confronting African-Americans in the late nineteenth century and to the World's Columbian Exposition as a monument to white supremacist values. Wells recited with grim preciseness the series of "political massacres" that occurred in the South following emancipation—the "midnight outrages of the Ku Klux Klans," discriminatory legislation that prevented African-Americans from voting, and the convict-lease system that reinstituted conditions similar to slavery. Barnett detailed the efforts African-Americans had made to obtain exhibit space at the fair and equitable representation on various administrative boards and how these efforts came to naught. Exposition managers, Barnett ruefully observed, spent over ninety thousand dollars for floats that were never used for the exposition's dedication exercises, but they refused to appropriate two thousand dollars for transporting African-American exhibits. "Theoretically open to all Americans," Barnett observed, the fair was "literally and figuratively, a 'White City,' in the building of which the Colored American was allowed no helping hand, and in its glorious success he has no share."[9]

Barnett was right. Exposition directors systematically excluded African-Americans from positions of responsibility (even from positions on the fair's police force) and turned the exposition into a cultural machine that reinforced prevailing racist stereotypes. But a handful of African-Americans exhibited at the fair, and some prominent African-American leaders appeared at fair-sponsored events. For instance, New York's J. Imogen Howard, the only African-American to serve on a state world's fair commission for the Chicago fair, received display space in the Woman's Building for her *New York Statistics*, a compendium of various literary and textile products by African-Americans, while George Washington Carver, then a college student in Iowa, won space among the Iowa exhibits for his painting *Yucca Glorioso*, which received honorable mention from the judges. And several black industrial colleges set up exhibits in the Liberal Arts Building.[10]

One black college exhibit, the display established by Atlanta University describing its educational mission, inspired a revealing poem in that university's official bulletin. The poem, written in 1893 by A. T. Worden, framed a line drawing of a young African-American woman:

Atlanta University, an African-American college, created one of the few exhibits at the fair by African-Americans, left. A poem printed in the university bulletin, below, raised fundamental questions about prevailing racial attitudes.

Behold in this calm face
The modern sphinx, with such a thoughtful mien
As bids us pause, when like a Frankenstein,
A nation dares create another race.[11]

From the perspective of many African-Americans, this is precisely what the World's Columbian Exposition signified—a veritable cultural Frankenstein.

During the Labor Congress, one of many conferences of authorities in different fields held in conjunction with the fair, several influential black leaders hammered this point home. Ida Wells and Frederick Douglass issued stinging critiques of black working conditions in the South. They were joined by the little-known principal of Tuskegee

This cartoon from **World's Fair Puck** *reinforced dominant stereotypes of Africans.*

Institute, Booker T. Washington, who similarly condemned the crop-lien system as "another form of slavery." But Washington insisted that this system "could not exist but for the ignorance of the negro." Where Douglass and Wells bored deeply into the ideological bedrock of the White City, questioning assumptions of white supremacy, Washington adopted a different strategy that placed blame on the victims.[12]

Two years later, Douglass would be dead, and Booker T. Washington would be in charge of the Negro Building at the 1895 Atlanta Cotton States and International Exposition. There Washington would deliver his famous accommodationist speech, endorsing the principle of separate-but-equal. The 1893 Chicago World's Columbian Exposition marked the rise of a new generation of black leaders, some of whom determined that it would be in the best interests of African-Americans to appease the monster so clearly in view at the White City of 1893.[13]

African-Americans were not alone in trying to resolve how best to convert the Chicago fair to their own purposes. Influential upper- and middle-class white women saw in the fair an opportunity to advance the causes of voting rights, domestic reform, and greater economic opportunity for women. Unlike African-Americans, white women, by virtue of prevailing Victorian beliefs, possessed moral, if not political, authority and were successful in achieving a measure of representation at the fair. But just as the issue of representation at the fair polarized African-Americans, plans for women's representation crystallized differences among white women over strategies for redressing gender inequality in American society.[14]

Building on their earlier experiences, women regarded the 1893 fair as an appropriate vehicle for advancing their political and social reform agendas. Beginning with the Civil War Sanitary Fairs and continuing through the world's fairs in Philadelphia and New Orleans, prominent reformers had relied on the exposition medium to build popular support for a variety of causes. What was unusual in the case of the World's Columbian Exposition was that the bill authorizing congressional support for the fair included a provision for the creation of a Board of Lady Managers.

The provision was the subject of disagreement among women. Supporters of the provision, including the wealthy women who served on the fair's powerful Auxiliary Executive Committee, saw the exposition as a primary site for advancing women's charity activities and domestic reform ideas. Critics, among them women professionals and suffragists, questioned the wisdom of a separate board of women fair managers and set up a rival Queen Isabella Society. As suffragist Susan B. Anthony argued the Isabellas' case in a petition presented to Congress, their goal was to include women in regular positions of world's fair management to assure that "there will be in the exhibition a presentation of the share taken by women in the industrial, artistic, intellectual, and religious progress of the nation." When Congress rejected Anthony's petition and instead established a separate Board of Lady Managers whose members would be selected by the male exposition directorate, the stage was set for a conflict.[15]

Left: The Woman's Building, designed by Sophia Hayden, housed exhibits by women and was used as a gathering place for women at the fair. Its existence symbolized the separate-but-equal treatment of women at the fair, a source of pride for some women and a disappointment for others.

In Victorian society, women were seen as the embodiment of culture and the conveyers of civilization. Artwork throughout the building emphasized the importance of women's domestic roles to the progress of society. Some works, such as this mural, above, by Lydia Emmet, entitled Art, Science, and Literature, elevated women's societal role beyond domesticity.

Above: As president of the Board of Lady Managers, Bertha Palmer led women in their efforts to be represented at the fair.

Right: Nineteen-year-old Alice Rideout was chosen from numerous entrants to be the official sculptor of the Woman's Building. *She is shown at work on the pediment, which depicted "woman's work in the various walks of life." Opposite: The library of the* Woman's Building, *which contained works written by women authors.*

That women succeeded in organizing exhibits was due largely to Bertha Palmer, wife of Chicago mercantilist Potter Palmer. Bertha Palmer had strongly supported the creation of the Board of Lady Managers and, after being appointed to head the board, took steps to isolate the more extreme supporters of the Isabella Society and to win others over through her insistence on integrating women's exhibits with men's exhibits in appropriate exhibition buildings. A masterful politician, she did not try to silence her critics; rather she sought to control the arena in which they voiced their concerns. To accomplish this goal, she helped organize a World's Congress of Representative Women that featured speakers presenting a variety of viewpoints on women's issues.[16]

While she was taking steps to neutralize her critics, Palmer endeavored, with less success, to win the support of the exposition's bosses. The men who ran the fair, the elite of Chicago's established mercantilist and emergent corporate leadership, while not hostile in principle to women's involvement in the fair, sought to restrict their activities to fund-raising and, when that became impossible, to subordinate women's voices to their own. For instance, exposition directors rejected out of hand Palmer's argument that men's and women's inventions should be integrated in appropriate exposition palaces and that women's exhibits should be explicitly labeled as such. Then, when, exposition directors refused to help finance the transportation of women's exhibits, Palmer reconciled herself to the same separate-but-equal rationalizations that African-Americans resorted to and agreed to concentrate the bulk of women's exhibits in a separate Woman's Building.[17]

That decision carried profound consequences. There can be no doubt that Palmer won inclusion for women in the exposition. But Palmer's accommodationist strategy had another side. It endorsed the exposition's racial calculus—a calculus that divided humanity into categories of civilization and savagery.[18]

For the white women who either supported Palmer from the start or who were won over to her position, their pride in the Woman's Building outweighed other concerns. After all, the building was designed by Sophia Hayden, the first woman to graduate from the Massachusetts Institute of

Technology's program in architectural design. Its interior and exterior exhibition spaces presented a formidable assortment of displays that gave women exhibitors an opportunity to advance a broad agenda of social reform. But, if, as Bertha Palmer claimed, the Board of Lady Managers' goal was to present "a complete picture" of the social condition of women, they fell short of the mark. As historian Frances K. Pohl explains, because the board insisted on applying "elite standards of quality to the work of all races and classes" and on displaying "products rather than processes," the Woman's Building included exhibits that "con-

formed to the Board's well-defined aesthetic, intellectual, and moral standards."[19]

Hayden's building design was itself a monument to the efforts by some women to feminize American culture. Her "Palace of the Fair Sex," as it was dubbed by one souvenir publication, emulated Italian Renaissance designs and fit perfectly into the broader beaux-arts patterns of the White City. The building's imposing exterior ornamentation, sculpted by Alice Rideout, projected a vision of women's occupations, with figures representing "Charity, Beneficence, Literature, Art, and Home Life" dominating the bas-relief over the main

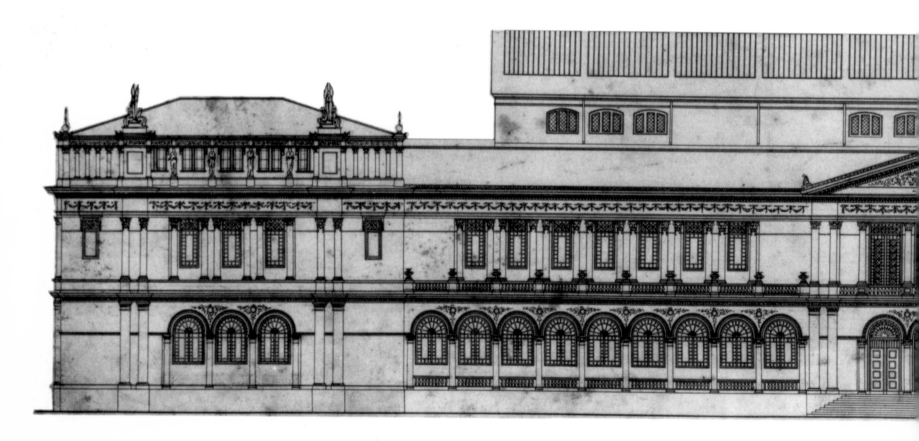

entrance. The overall effect was decidedly "feminine," possessing, in the words of architect Henry Van Brunt, "a certain quality of sentiment, which might be designated as . . . graceful timidity or gentleness, combined, however, with evident technical knowledge, which at once reveals the sex of its author." Or as one of the women managers described it: "Our building is essentially feminine in character: it has the qualities of reserve, delicacy, and refinement. . . . Its strength is veiled in grace; its beauty is gently impressive."[20]

Within and beyond the building, as historian Mary Cordato has recently noted, exhibits organized by women expanded the constraints of prevailing Victorian attitudes to embrace a broad range of social reform issues, including public health care, public housing, and education. Visitors could examine model hospital wards, walk through a model home for a working-class family, and study the latest advances in elementary and secondary education. In addition to the Woman's Building, the Board of Lady Managers sponsored a women's dormitory building near the exposition grounds to protect visiting women from the violence of the city and a Children's Building on the fairgrounds to demonstrate the latest theories about raising

The Woman's Building stood at the gateway to the Midway. In the eyes of the exposition's organizers, women came close to slipping into the category of "otherness" reserved for "savages" and "exotics."

the nation's young. Other exhibits, including displays devoted to women inventors and artists, bore witness to the message that the ideology of domesticity could fuel reforms that would improve women's economic and social opportunities.[21]

The ideology of domesticity gained visual representation in Mary Cassatt's mural, entitled *Modern Woman*, which decorated the south wall of the main hall in the Woman's Building. Cassatt divided her painting into three panels, with *The Arts, Music, and Dancing* and *Young Girls Pursuing Fame* framing

the centerpiece: *Young Women Plucking the Fruits of Knowledge and Science*. As summarized by one historian, Cassatt's mural reflected her "commitment to see in women's everyday activities humanity's highest aspirations." Put in slightly different terms, women's domestic sphere contained the seeds of "civilization."[22]

The importance of the domestic sphere for advancing civilization was also the message of Mary Fairchild MacMonnies's heroic narrative mural, which was located directly across the main hall from Cassatt's work. Entitled *Primitive Woman*, the mural had been commissioned by Bertha Palmer to complement *Modern Woman*. Historian Jeanne Weimann aptly describes the murals: Primitive woman "crushed grapes and carried water, burdened by a babe in arms. Modern woman picked fruit, plucked a lyre, and gracefully pursued an Ideal." In the Woman's Building as in the exposition as a whole, pursuit of the civilized ideal required the representation of its counterpoint—savagery.[23]

As if to underscore that message, the Woman's Building was located in the northwest corner of the White City, at the gateway to the Midway Plaisance, the mile-long avenue that combined amusement with ethnological instruction about people who were typed as exotic or savage. The effect of crossing from the Midway to the White City was captured by novelist Clara Louisa Burnham in *Sweet Clover*: "You know that in what seemed like one step, you've passed out o' darkness and into light." Looking up at the angels on the Woman's Building, Burnham's fictional fairgoers could feel elevated by the progress they had made from the chaos associated with the Midway to the order symbolized by the White City.[24]

There was, of course, another message in this ideologically laden mapping of the exposition grounds. If the position of the Woman's Building right at the doorstep of the Midway was any indication, women, in the eyes of the exposition's male sponsors, came close to slipping into the category of "otherness" reserved for "savages" and "exotics." They were redeemed only by their capacity to serve as mothers of civilization—a stereotype that some upper- and middle-class white women were only too happy to embrace to advance their own reform agenda. As a result, women's representation at the World's Columbian Exposition recapitulated and reinforced prevailing sentiments of white supremacy.

As enraged as African-Americans may have been over their treatment by exposition authorities and as compromised as many women may have felt by the concessions they were forced to make to secure representation in the fair, these groups had a measure of political and moral standing in American society and could make themselves heard. That task was more difficult for Native Americans and nonwhites from other cultures who were put on display in what the official exhibit classification referred to as "Department M," but what was better known as the Midway Plaisance.

With its towering, revolving wheel, designed by engineer George Ferris, lifting visitors 260 feet above the exposition grounds, the Midway has been remembered as an entertainment strip. But, in addition to its amusements, the Midway also boasted so-called ethnological villages, modeled after similar displays at the 1889 Paris Exposition Universelle, which had been located near the base of the Eiffel Tower. Chicago's exposition

The 260-foot-high Ferris Wheel came to symbolize not only the Midway, but the entire exposition.

Despite the heat of a Chicago summer, members of the Innuit tribe, referred to at the fair as Esquimaux, were expected to perform with their huskies while dressed in the fur garments of their native land. When the concessionaires threatened to withhold food, some of the Innuits sued them and were released from their contract. Opposite: Photograph by C. D. Arnold.

directors knew that French colonial villages had been enormously profitable. Given the precarious financial condition of the World's Columbian Exposition, these shows gained added appeal for exposition organizers. But how could such shows be included without detracting from the refinements of the White City? The Paris example showed the way. At the 1889 fair, leading anthropologists had given their blessing to the colonial villages as authentic replications of native life and treated them as ethnological field camps. Chicago's exposition builders went one better. They placed one of America's leading ethnologists, Frederic Ward Putnam of Harvard, in charge of Department M, home of the fair's anthropology displays as well as its Midway amusements. Fair planners used these ethnological villages to support one of the central messages of the fair, namely, that the progress of Western civilization could be measured by comparing "less civilized" people to white Americans.[25]

In recent years, much has been written about the Midway Plaisance: how it "commodified the exotic"; how its ethnological intentions were subverted by its commercial prospects; and how it helped sow the seeds for popular support for American imperial adventures later in the decade.[26] But the motives and reactions of the people put on display are less clear. The people who endured exploitive conditions were not just passive victims of world's fair authorities, entrepreneurial anthropologists, and mercenary concessionaires. Some of the people put on display knowingly complied with the strategies of exposition sponsors; others contested their representation as bottom rungs on a living ladder of humanity.

The Esquimaux village was one case in point. Situated in the extreme northwest corner of the exposition grounds, several hundred yards from the Midway, the village consisted of about sixty Innuits. It was one of the first ethnological exhibits established at the exposition. Before the Innuits arrived in Chicago, the entrepreneur responsible for organizing the show had promised them "$100,00, 200 lbs. salt, 30 lbs. rice, 20 gallons of molasses, 10 lbs. tea, 200 cartridges, a Winchester rifle, one reloading outfit, 20 lbs. powder, 20 lbs. shot, 80 lbs. lead, 1000 explosive caps, one barrel of pork, 3 barrels of flour, one barrel of pilot bread, and numerous other smaller articles" in exchange for their participation. The Innuits were to arrive in Chicago in the autumn of 1892, long before the official opening of the fair, to give them a chance to adjust to the climate. But the Innuits—including a newborn baby named Christopher Columbus—were immediately put on display before crowds that paid to see them perform with their huskies and kayaks and live out their daily lives in overcrowded cabins and bark huts.[27]

Conditions for the Innuits grew worse. In February, poor food—whether it was spoiled or lacking in quantity is unclear—and the absence of fresh water, together with cramped living quarters, led one of the Innuits to seize the concessionaire's interpreter and give him "a good shaking." Police restored order, and the manager of the village told the Innuits they were his "chattels." In April, when one of the villagers refused to wear a fur coat because it made him too hot, the concessionaire ordered exposition police to arrest him. According to press reports, the concessionaire told the villager: "Wear fur clothes or you get no food." Five

Native Americans also petitioned for representation at the fair. Instead, they experienced degrading exploitation as exhibits on the Midway.

Right: Penobscot wigwams. Photograph by C. D. Arnold.

Below: A life mask of Chief Rain-in-the-Face, a Sioux who was one of the original petitioners.

Innuit families immediately hired an attorney and sued the concessionaire. They complained of being held "practically as prisoners." Convinced of the legitimacy of their case, the court released the complainants from their contract. The Innuit who had earlier assaulted the interpreter found employment as a carpenter for $350 a year—a substantial increase over the $50 he would have earned for performing at the fair—while several others set up their own show amidst the honky-tonk concessions that had sprung up outside the exposition grounds.[28]

The efforts by some Innuits to control their working conditions were not unique. When the fair was in its early planning stages, several Native Americans wrote the U.S. commissioner of Indian affairs: "We, American citizens of Indian blood, most earnestly and respectfully petition you to grant us through the forthcoming World's Fair and anniver-

sary of the discovery of America, some recognition as a race; some acknowledgement that we are still a part, however inferior, of America and the Great American Republic." Specifically, the Native Americans asked for the opportunity to develop their own exhibits. "With a Native American, or Indian exhibit in the hands of capable men of our own blood . . . ," the petitioners insisted, "a most interesting and instructive and surely successful feature will be added . . . [that] will show to both and all races alike, that our own advancement has been much greater than is usually supposed." The petitioners added: "Give us . . . some reason to be glad with you that [America] was so discovered."[29]

United States government officials and world's fair authorities were only too happy to include representations of Native Americans—especially since the popular Buffalo Bill's Wild West Show, located outside the fairgrounds, would compete with Midway shows—but not on terms set by the petitioners. World's fair managers awarded an American Indian village concession to showmen Thomas Roddy and Henry "Buckskin Joe" De Ford, who proceeded to organize sixty Native Americans drawn from different tribal groups into a Midway display. Exposition directors also awarded another Native American show to Wild West entrepreneur, P. B. Wickham. Called "Sitting Bull's Cabin," this exhibit featured nine Sioux, including Chief Rain-in-the-Face, one of the original petitioners to the government for control of Native American representations.[30]

Instead of dignified representation, Native Americans experienced degrading exploitation. In one memorable performance in the Indian village, Chief Twobites and Joe Strongback removed their shirts while the interpreter for the concession "produced a keen knife and two pieces of rope and cut four deep gashes in the back of each Indian between the shoulder blades. Then raising the quivering flesh he passed the ends of the rope beneath the skin and tied them in hard."[31]

Regarded and treated as subhuman, some Native Americans on display turned to alcohol and violence, fighting with each other and show managers. Others probably contented themselves with the money they earned. If historian of anthropology Lester George Moses is right, Native Americans may have made some contractual gains by forcing showmen to negotiate with performers as individuals. But the overall response of Native Americans to the fair was anticipated by the signators of the original petition to the United States government for control over their representation at the fair. "The people[?] are almost despairing," the petitioners wrote, "and it is inevitable that our people trace the causes of that despairing and consequently desperate condition to the very event which, with such large expenditures of wealth, you are about to celebrate."[32]

The responses of another group displayed on the Midway, the Dahomeyans, are even more difficult to reconstruct. Inspired by the tremendous success of French colonial shows at the 1889 fair, Chicago's exposition builders created a Dahomeyan village under the control of Xavier Pené, an intrepid African explorer and a labor contractor who had supplied workers for the construction of the Pan-American Railroad in the 1880s. This imperial conqueror-turned-showman brought about seventy Africans to the fair, where they lived in habitat dwellings that had been constructed by local laborers before the Dahomeyans arrived. They performed an assort-

Left: King Bull's Tipee Hut, one of the features in the Native American show that housed nine Sioux, operated by Wild West entrepreneur P. B. Wickham.

Below left: The Sioux Lone Dog. This photograph from Midway Types *was labeled "A Gentleman of Leisure."*

Below: A woman tourist strolling through one of the Native American villages.

ment of dances that generally reinforced the negative opinion given by one guidebook: "The habits of
these people are repulsive; they eat like animals
and have all the characteristics of the very lowest
order of the human family. Nearly all the women
are battle-scarred; most of them are captives."[33]

The lives of the Dahomeyans at the fair were no
better than those of the Innuits. One newspaper
noted that "the Dahomeyans were practically
slaves. They got nothing but their board, the consideration of their services being paid to their chief
at home." When his wards gave him trouble, Pené
plied them with "lavish use of beer" and encouraged them to dance with pint bottles. But, as did
the Innuits and Native Americans, Dahomeyans
resisted their exposition masters. In her pioneer-
ing study of various Midway village performances,
Gertrude M. Scott quotes the Austrian village manager's observations of the Dahomeyan women,
who were forced to parade through the Midway
along with other Midway performers.

A good many people imagine, I suppose, [that the
African women] are sounding the praises of the
Exposition or at least voicing their wonder at the
marvels they have seen since coming to this country. But the fact is that if the words of their chants
were translated into English they would read something like this: "We have come from a far country to
a land where all men are white. If you will come to
our country we will take pleasure in cutting your
white throats."

This tale, as Scott points out, may well have been
apocryphal, but, given the actions of other Midway performers to take control over the condi-

tions of their representation, it could easily contain a kernel of truth.[34]

Many people featured as Midway specimens manifested various strategies of resistance to preserve their dignity. The conditions that necessitated that resistance were not simply material, but ideological, following a system of beliefs embedded in the exposition that typed some people as "other." This "orientalist" structure of thought that pervaded the Midway crystallized in a cluster of exhibits—the Street in Cairo, the Algerian Village, the Persian Palace, the Wild East Show, the Moorish Palace, and the Turkish Theater—that were among the most popular attractions along the Midway.

Modeled on similar shows at previous European fairs that were intended to reinforce the imperial designs of European countries, these displays at the Chicago fair gave the Midway its distinctive, "exotic" look. As one journalist described the scene:

Everybody went first to the Midway Plaisance. And what a picture that road down the center presented. Sunday or no Sunday, you met people of all nations, all stations, all classes and all dressed in holiday

Below left: The "exotic" displays of Eastern cultures perpetuated an image of underdevelopment in comparison to industrialized nations, which served to reinforce America's imperial ambitions and policies. Vital to this strategy was the portrayal of Middle Eastern women as sexually alluring.

Opposite: Burros on the Street in Cairo. Photograph by Lekegian and Co. Below right: Camels and their riders from the Wild East Show.

Right: The Algerian village.
Photograph by C. D. Arnold.
Opposite: The Street in
Cairo. Photograph by
C. D. Arnold.

In contrast to the Oriental
and Native American
villages, the folkloric Euro-
pean villages portrayed cul-
tures capable of assimilating
into American society.
Right: The German village.
Photograph by C. D. Arnold.

attire. There were Turks in European costume, with red fez, and Turks in all the glory of rich silk turbans, purple silk mantles and yellow silk trousers; Arabs in long, pale, tan-colored robes, embroidered in gold, and in long silk robes, covered with gold lace.

Together with camels, donkeys, and distinctive architectural designs, the "oriental" displays seemed authentic. But, as architectural historians Zeynep Çelik and Leila Kinney have argued, these villages played a specific purpose. "The fabricated streets, shops, artisans, and merchants," they write, "created a visible difference from the industrialized nations." The overall effect was not simply to amuse, but to perpetuate an image of underdevelopment—an image perfectly suited to nurturing the imperial ambitions of exposition sponsors on both sides of the Atlantic.[35]

Vital to this strategy, as Çelik and Kinney argue, was the representation of Middle Eastern women. At the 1893 fair, concessionaires, who included prominent Chicago businessmen and their Middle Eastern counterparts, replicated one of the most popular attractions from the 1889 Paris exposition—the belly dance. Generally referred to as the "danse du ventre" because, as one journalist noted, the translation would "sound ill in American ears," it was performed in four theaters on the Midway by a variety of performers, but apparently not, as it has been commonly assumed, by anyone known as "Little Egypt." One account captured the lure of the dance: the dancer "revels in all the glory of oriental colors and barbaric jewelry and there it is she displays her charms, dimly hidden by a gauze nothing; a narrow zone of gauze silk though which the warm flesh tints are distinctly visible." In at least one theater, the Per-

Many Chicagoans in 1893 lived and worked in unsanitary and unsafe conditions. Industrial accidents could kill or maim workers.

Opposite: An immigrant injured in an industrial accident. Over thirty workers died building the fair.

sian Palace of Eros, the audience was exclusively male and routinely made lewd comments about the dancers, who concluded their performance by doing the splits. Evocative of erotic fantasies, the dances, as Çelik and Kinney suggest, constituted "models of possession" that "anchor[ed] colonial power at the individual level."[36]

But this was not their sole effect. At the same time that these dances supported the Midway's exotic qualities, they had a contradictory, subversive effect on prudish Victorian sexual attitudes. It was precisely this realization that led the clergy and the Board of Lady Managers to launch a crusade to close the theaters—a crusade that, given the profitability of the shows, exposition authorities were reluctant to support. In the battle for the soul of American culture, as historian James Gilbert has noted, the erotically charged commercialism of the Midway constantly threatened the overcivilized values of the White City. At every turn, it seemed, the energies unleashed by the Palace of Eros threatened to overwhelm the plaster-of-paris palaces of the White City.[37]

But those commercial and erotic energies were constrained by an iron cage of race. The presentation of white European ethnic groups stood in sharp contrast to the "exotic" cultures of the Orient. The Irish village, for instance, demonstrated that "Irish poverty will be cured by Irish industry," while the German village, operated by the immigration agent for the Atchison, Topeka, and Santa Fe Railroad, seemed bent on creating the impression that German immigrants were wholly capable of assimilating into American society. Threatened as it may have been by the raw energies of the Midway, the White City was not without its defenses,

chief of which was its insistence on *herrenvolk* values of racial exclusivity.[38]

Politically and culturally correct by the standards of an age characterized by the relentless search for overseas empire, the Chicago World's Columbian Exposition manifested another characteristic of imperialism—disease. The exposition's most immediate bequest to the city of Chicago was not its architecture, mass entertainment, or insistence upon civic reform, but a smallpox epidemic that added another layer of despair to the panic caused by the economic depression that hit in the summer of 1893. As Chicago's commissioner of public health noted: "It is fair to assume that smallpox was one of the things the fair brought to Chicago." Before it ran its course in 1894, the epidemic claimed 1,213 lives.[39]

How exactly did the fair precipitate an epidemic? Historian of medicine Thomas Neville Bonner describes the general social conditions prevalent in Chicago at the time of the fair: "At the time Chicago was receiving the world's plaudits at the Columbian Exposition in 1893, it had already outdistanced other cities in the misery and degradation of its citizens." More specifically, health conditions at the fairgrounds and living conditions for workers—many of them European immigrants—employed to construct the exposition's buildings were deplorable. During the construction period, there were 5,919 medical and surgical cases reported by the exposition's medical department. Over thirty workers died building the fair; of these many died of fractured skulls. No less dramatic were the outbreaks of typhoid fever, diarrhea, and bronchitis that raged during the construction of the fair. One former worker, who

In the immigrant district of Chicago, a smallpox epidemic broke out after the fair.

later became a professor at Princeton and had largely positive recollections of his life as a laborer at the fair, let slip that more than four hundred workers were forced to live and eat together in one building where they were guarded by sentries—evidently to keep them from contact with union organizers. Given that Chicago had not had a smallpox vaccination program for nearly a decade, what were intended as model dormitories for workers quickly became microbial compression chambers. Then, once the fair was built, thousands of immigrant workers remained in Chicago, often unemployed and living in circumstances that worsened with the onset of the depression. Conditions quickly ripened for a catastrophic outbreak of disease.[40]

The state of the ethnological villages during the fair compounded the already virulent situation of the period preceding the exposition. On the eve of the fair's opening, an attorney for the management of the Turkish village, in a revealing use of language, told the press that the "inmates of the Turkish village are in a wretched condition." He complained that "the sanitary arrangements are something horrible," noting that there was not one public toilet on the entire Midway. There should have been additional cause for concern when it took public health officials nearly seven weeks to quarantine the Innuits after an outbreak of measles.[41]

The consequences of neglect hit towards the end of the world's fair season. Between August and November 1893, smallpox cases reached epidemic proportions. The effects were immediately felt in the city's Emergency Isolation Hospital, more popularly known as the "pesthouse." As the *Chicago Tribune* later recalled:

In that winter [of 1893–94] following the world's fair the Chicago pesthouse was a hideous structure in itself, through which 3,500 cases passed. Far into the summer the epidemic ran and the buildings back of bridewell were so filled with the afflicted that ropes were stretched, soldiers established a 'dead' line, and tents were set up to accommodate those crowded out of the building.

Linked causally with the exposition, the epidemic took an extraordinary toll among the powerless, especially among children, foreign workers, and Midway villagers who had been left to fend for themselves once the exposition closed.[42]

In this tragedy there was no small measure of irony. For more surely than any exhibit at the fair, the epidemic occasioned by the World's Columbian Exposition confirmed the claims by exposition builders that they stood on Columbus's shoulders. Marked by the pox that Columbus and his voyagers introduced to the New World, the World's Columbian Exposition was more true to its distant origins than its organizers had ever dreamed possible.[43]

Commenting several decades later on the architectural legacy of the World's Columbian Exposition, architect Louis Sullivan, who designed the Transportation Building, observed that the fair had "penetrated deep into the constitution of the American mind, effecting there lesions significant of dementia." Lesions there may have been, but the architecture was only symptomatic of deeper flaws in the guiding vision that directed the fair. Deeply inscribed with prevailing beliefs about race and gender, the exposition posited a common culture for some Americans at the expense of others. Con-

sequently, it occasioned great skepticism and outrage from people who were either excluded from the fair or included only to be treated as subordinates. As a cultural and political battleground over the future direction of American society, the World's Columbian Exposition revealed tensions that would continue to haunt the United States far into the next century.[44]

NOTES

I am grateful to the staff of the Chicago Historical Society for their support of this project. Wim de Wit and Connie Casey went beyond the call of duty in supplying information. Pam Harkins was very resourceful in working through medical records in the city of Chicago.

1. Much has been written about the 1893 Chicago World's Columbian Exposition. Interested readers should start with: R. Reid Badger, *The Great American Fair: The World's Columbian Exposition and American Culture* (Chicago: Nelson-Hall, 1979); David F. Burg, *Chicago's White City of 1893* (Lexington, KY: University of Kentucky Press, 1976); James Gilbert, *Perfect Cities: Chicago's Utopias of 1893* (Chicago: University of Chicago Press, 1991); Neil Harris, *Cultural Excursions: Marketing Appetites and Cultural Tastes in Modern America* (Chicago: University of Chicago Press, 1990); Thomas S. Hines, *Burnham of Chicago: Architect and Planner* (New York: Oxford University Press, 1974); Helen Lefkowitz Horowitz, *Culture and the City: Cultural Philanthrophy in Chicago from the 1880s to 1917* (Lexington, KY: University of Kentucky Press, 1976), and Robert Rydell, *All the World's a Fair: Visions of Empire at American International Expositions, 1876–1916* (Chicago: University of Chicago Press, 1984), ch. 2.

2. Rydell, ch. 2.

3. Ann Massa, "Black Women in the 'White City,'" *Journal of American Studies* 8 (1974): 319–37; "The Women and the World's Fair," *New York Age*, Oct. 24, 1891; Elliot M. Rudwick and August Meier, "Black Man in the 'White City,'" *Phylon* 26 (1965): 358. See also Dreck Spurlock Wilson, "Black Involvement in Chicago's Previous World's Fairs," unpublished paper, 1984, Chicago Historical Society Library, vertical files (cited hereafter as CHS).

4. Details of this controversy are presented by Rydell, 52–53; Rudwick and Meier, 359–61; Wilson, 12–14; and Alfreda M. Duster, ed., *Crusade for Justice: The Autobiography of Ida B. Wells* (Chicago: University of Chicago Press, 1970), 118–19.

5. "The Jubilee Day Folly," *Indianapolis Freeman*, Sept. 2, 1893.

6. William McFeely, *Frederick Douglass* (New York: W. W. Norton, 1991), 370–72, provides a fine description of the day's events. Douglass quoted in "The World in Miniature," *Indianapolis Freeman*, Sept. 2, 1893; and, "Appeal of Douglass," *Chicago Tribune*, Aug. 26, 1893.

7. Wells quoted in McFeely, 371.

8. Frederick Douglass, Ida Wells, and Ferdinand Barnett, *The*

Reason Why. The Colored American Is Not in the World's Columbian Exposition (no imprint, 1893), 2–3.

9.   Douglass, Wells, and Barnett, 13, 75, 79.

10. Wilson, 11.

11. *The Bulletin of Atlanta University* 48 (July 1893): 1, 8. CHS clipping file.

12. "An Account of a Speech before the Labor Congress, Chicago," Sept. 2, 1893, *Booker T. Washington Papers*, ed. Louis R. Harlan, vol. 3 (Urbana, IL: University of Illinois Press, 1974), 364–65.

13. Regarding Washington's involvement with the 1895 fair, see Rydell, 82–85.

14. The role of women at the 1893 fair has attracted growing attention. In addition to Jeanne Madeline Weimann's *The Fair Women* (Chicago: Academy Chicago, 1981), readers should consult: Frances K. Pohl, "Historical Reality of Utopian Ideal?" *International Journal of Women's Studies* 5 (1982): 289–311; Virginia Grant Darney, "Women and World's Fairs: American International Expositions, 1876–1904," Ph.D. diss. (Emory University, 1982); and Mary Frances Cordato, "Representing the Expansion of Woman's Sphere: Women's Work and Culture at the World's Fairs of 1876, 1893, and 1904," Ph.D. diss., (New York University, 1989).

15. Anthony quoted in Weimann, 36. Details concerning the controversy besetting the Board of Lady Managers and its creation are provided by Weimann, Pohl, and Cordato, passim.

16. Cordato, 216–24; Weimann, 73–101.

17. *Addresses and Reports of Mrs. Potter Palmer* (Chicago: Rand McNally, 1894), 125. See also Cordato, 228–33.

18. Pohl, 296–97, lays the basis for this claim.

19. Pohl, 298.

20. Judith Paine, "Sophia Hayden and the Woman's Building," *Helicon Nine* 1 (Fall/Winter 1979), 28–37. The Columbian Gallery and Henry Van Brunt quoted in ibid, 32, 34, 36. See also Maud Howe Elliott, ed., *Art and Handicraft in the Woman's Building of the World's Columbian Exposition* (Paris: Goupil and Co., 1893), 25.

21. See Cordato, passim.

22. Sally Webster, "Mary Cassatt's Allegory of Modern Woman," *Helicon Nine* 1 (Fall/Winter 1979), 38–47.

23. Weimann, 214.

24. Clara Louisa Burnham, *Sweet Clover* (Chicago: Laird and Lee, 1893), 201.

25. Rydell, 60–68.

26. Curtis M. Hinsley, "The World as Marketplace: Commodification of the Exotic at the World's Columbian Exposition, Chicago, 1893," in *Exhibiting Cultures: The Poetics and Politics of Museum Display*, Ivan Karp and Steven D. Lavine, eds. (Washington, D.C.: Smithsonian Institution Press, 1991), 363.

27. "Esquimaux Must Not Be Detained," *Chicago Mail*, Apr. 3, 1893; Gertrude M. Scott, "Village Performance: Villages of the Chicago World's Columbian Exposition of 1893," Ph.D. diss. (New York University, 1990), 312–26; *Chicago Times Portfolio of Midway Types*, part 2 (Chicago: American Eng. Co. Publishers and Printers, 1893), n.p.

28. "The Fighting Esquimau," *Illustrated World's Fair* 4 (Feb. 1893): 443; "Javanese are Bowed with Grief," *Chicago Mail*, Apr. 21, 1893; "The Eskimos are Out," *The Bee*, Apr. 29, 1893.

29. "To the Commissioners of the Columbian Exposition," 1891[?], Frederic Ward Putnam Papers, Box 34, Harvard University Archives.

30. L. G. Moses, "Indians on the Midway: Wild West Shows and the Indian Bureau at World's Fairs, 1893–1904," *South Dakota History* 21 (1991): 220; Scott, 326–34.

31. Moses writes on p. 217: "Indians may also have been abused and ridiculed, but neither the newspaper accounts nor the agency records that contain comments by and about Indians bears this out. Finally, how is one to judge whether or not Indians benefited from participation in the exhibition? Some may just have had a good time. It would be better to examine that topic from the perspective of the Indians themselves." Cf. "Stop the Horrid Torture Dances," *Chicago Tribune*, Aug. 20, 1893, 12; and "Return as Freaks: Descendants of Chicago's Original Settlers Come to Town," *Chicago Tribune*, July 1, 1893, 1.

32. Scott, 328–29; Moses, 219–20; "To the Commissioners of the Columbian Exposition," op. cit.

33. Rydell, 145–46; Scott, 283–303, John J. Flinn, comp., *Official Guide to Midway Plaisance* (Chicago: The Columbian Guide Company, [1893]), 30.

34. [Unidentified newspaper clipping], Charles Harpel Scrapbooks, Manuscripts Division, CHS; Scott, 297–98.

35. Teresa Dean, *White City Chips* (Chicago: Warren Publishing Co., 1895), 15; Zeynep Çelik and Leila Kinney, "Ethnography and Exhibitionism at the Expositions Universelles," *Assemblages* 13 (1986): 39. See also, Edward Said, *Orientalism* (New York: Random House, 1979); and Timothy Mitchell, "The World as Exhibition," *Comparative Studies in Society and History* 31 (1989): 217–36.

36. Çelik and Kinney, passim, 46; "Danse De [sic] Ventre on the Plaisance," *Chicago Mail*, June 3, 1893. On the controversy over "Little Egypt," see Scott, 195–213.

37. Gilbert, 130.

38. Frank H. Smith, *Art History, Midway Plaisance and World's Fair* (Chicago: Foster Press, 1893), n.p. On the centrality of *herrenvolk* concepts of race to late nineteenth-century America, see George Frederickson, *Black Image in the White Mind: The Debate on Afro-American Character and Destiny, 1817–1914* (New York: Harper Torchbooks, 1971).

39. Arthur R. Reynolds, "History of the Chicago Smallpox Epidemic of 1893, 1894, and 1895. . . ," in *The Rise and Fall of Disease in Illinois*, ed. Isaac R. Rawlings (Springfield, IL,: n.p., 1927), 313. Additional information about the epidemic can be found in *Annual Report of the Department of Health of the City of Chicago for the Year Ended December 31, 1894* (Chicago: n.p., 1895).

40. Thomas Neville Bonner, *Medicine in Chicago, 1850–1950: A Chapter in the Social and Scientific Development of a City* (Urbana, IL: University of Illinois Press, 1991), 20; "Report of the Medical Department. World's Columbian Exposition," n.d., Chicago Public Library; Walter A. Wyckoff, *The Workers: An Experiment in Reality* (New York: Charles Scribners and Sons, 1917), 248.

41. "May Breed Disease at the Fair," *Chicago Mail*, May 25, 1893; Dean, 7.

42. "No Epidemic of Smallpox," *Chicago Tribune*, Feb. 3, 1901, 43, clipping, CHS, vertical files, f. "Smallpox."

43. Alfred A. Crosby, *The Columbian Exchange: Biological and Cultural Consequences of 1492* (Westport, CT.: Greenwood Press,1972).

44. Louis Sullivan, *The Autobiography of an Idea* (New York: W. W. Norton, 1926), 325.

ILLUSTRATION CREDITS

ICHi-25220; 53 right, The Getty Center for the History of Art and the Humanities, Special Collections; 54, CHS, ICHi-25217; 55, from *The Architecture of John Welborn Root* (1973), CHS Library; 56, CHS, ICHi-25036; 57, top four, Courtesy of The Art Institute of Chicago, The Architects Portrait Collection; 57 bottom left, CHS, ICHi-23641; 59, CHS, ICHi-25050; 60, CHS, ICHi-17121; 61, CHS, ICHi-25144; 62, Lawrence Public Library, Lawrence, MA; 63, CHS, ICHi-25169; 64 top, CHS, ICHi-25192; 64 bottom, CHS, ICHi-25191; 65, CHS, ICHi-25193; 66 top left, CHS, ICHi-25135; 66 bottom left and right, Courtesy, Field Museum of Natural History; 67 top, CHS, ICHi-17122; 67 bottom, CHS Archives and Manuscripts Collection; 68 top, CHS, ICHi-17531; 68 bottom, CHS, ICHi-23178; 69; CHS, ICHi-17530; 70, CHS, ICHi-23185; 71 top, CHS, ICHi-25037; 71 bottom, CHS, ICHi-25032; 72, CHS, ICHi-17137; 73, CHS Charles F. Murphy Architectural Study Center Collection; 74, from *The Century World's Fair Book*, CHS Library; 75, CHS, ICHi-25043; 76, CHS, ICHi-25216; 77, CHS, ICHi-25199; 78, CHS, ICHi-02539; 79 top, CHS, ICHi-25195; 79 bottom left, CHS, ICHi-25213; 79 bottom right, CHS, 25212; 80, CHS, ICHi-25215; 81 top, CHS, ICHi-13655; 81 bottom, CHS, ICHi-25210; 82, CHS, ICHi-25206; 83 left, CHS, ICHi-25207; 83 right, The Getty Center for the History of Art and the Humanities; 84, CHS, ICHi-02502; 85, CHS, ICH-02526; 86, CHS, ICHi-25052; 87 top, CHS, ICHi-25211; 87 bottom, CHS, ICHi-25194; 88 left, CHS Prints and Photographs Collection; 88 right, CHS, ICHi-25228; 89, CHS, ICHi-25000; 90 top, CHS, ICHi-23166; 90 bottom, CHS, ICHi-23346; 91, CHS, ICHi-25084; 92, CHS, ICHi-25049; 93 top; CHS, ICHi-22868; 93 bottom, CHS Prints and Photographs Collection; 94, CHS, ICHi-25143; 95, CHS, ICHi-25202.

FIXING THE IMAGE

100, CHS, ICHi-25057; 101, Doug Fymbo; 102, CHS, ICHi-23350; 103, CHS, ICHi-23352; 104 top, CHS Library; 104 bottom, from *New York at the World's Columbian Exposition* (1894), CHS Library; 105, CHS, ICHi-25161; 106 top, CHS, ICHi-25017; 106 bottom, CHS, ICHi-25013; 107 top, CHS, ICHi-25042; 107 bottom, CHS, ICHi-25235; 108, CHS Prints and Photographs Collection; 109 top, CHS, ICHi-25196; 109 bottom, Steve Frank, Rochelle, IL; 110, CHS, ICHi-13854; 111 top, CHS, ICHi-25157; 111 bottom, CHS, ICHi-25111; 112 top and bottom, private collection of Mr. and Mrs. Harlow Niles Higinbotham; 113, CHS, ICHi-25058; 114, CHS, ICHi-25053; 115, CHS, ICHi-17532; 116 top, from *Midway Types*, CHS Library; 116 bottom, CHS, ICHi-25109; 117, CHS, ICHi-25088; 118 top, CHS, ICHi-17136; 118 bottom, CHS, ICHi-25131; 119, CHS, ICHi-25112; 120, CHS, ICHi-02211; 121 top, CHS, ICHi-25092; 121 bottom, CHS, ICHi-25110; 122, CHS, ICHi-25128; 123 top, from *Official Views of the World's Columbian Exposition*, CHS Library; 123 bottom, CHS, ICHi-25236; 124, CHS, ICHi-25171; 125 left, CHS, ICHi-25166; 125 right, CHS, ICHi-25125; 126, CHS, ICHi-25087, 127 top, CHS, ICHi-25237; 127 bottom, Cleveland Public Library, Cleveland, OH; 128, CHS, ICHi-25115; 129, CHS, ICHi-25106; 130, CHS, ICHi-25091.

COLOR PLATES

133, CHS Prints and Photographs Collection; 134 left, CHS, ICHi-25164, 134 right, CHS Prints and Photographs; 135, CHS Hope B. McCormick Costume Collection; 136, CHS Library; 137 left, ICHI-06181; 137 right, CHS Library; 138 left top, ICHi-25189; 138 left bottom, ICHi-25188; 138 right, ICHi-25184; 139, CHS Library; 140, CHS Painting and Sculpture Collection.

A CULTURAL FRANKENSTEIN?

142, CHS, ICHi-25062; 144, CHS, ICHi-10139; 145, CHS, ICHi-25126; 146, from *Midway Types*, CHS Library; 147, from *World's Fair Puck*, October 2, 1893; 148, Private Collection of Donald Duster; 149 top and bottom, Atlanta University Center, Robert W. Woodruff Library, Archives and Special Collections, Atlanta, GA 30314; 150, CHS, ICHi-25175; 151 left, CHS, ICHi-16265; 151 right, CHS, ICHi-02312; 152 left, CHS, ICHi-25223; 152 right, CHS, ICHi-02388; 153, CHS, ICHi-25099; 154, CHS Charles F. Murphy Architectural Study Center Collection; 155, CHS, ICHi-02308; 156, CHS Prints and Photographs Collection; 157, CHS, ICHi-25123; 158, CHS, ICHi-25198; 159, CHS, ICHi-18781; 160 top, CHS, ICHi-19615; 160 bottom, William Hammond Mathers Museum, Bloomington, IN; 161 top, CHS, ICHi-25113; 161 bottom left, from *Midway Types*, CHS Library; 161 bottom right, CHS, ICHi-25234; 162, CHS, ICHi-25141; 163 left, CHS, ICHi-23443; 163 right, CHS, ICHi-25116; 164 top, CHS, ICHi-16916; 164 bottom, CHS, ICHi-25173; 165, CHS, ICHi-25117; 166, University of Illinois at Chicago, The University Library, Jane Addams Memorial Collection; 167, CHS, ICHi-21975; 168, University of Illinois at Chicago, The University Library, Jane Addams Memorial Collection; 169, CHS Library.

INDEX

Illustrations are indicated with underlines. If a subject is illustrated and discussed on the same page, the illustration is not separately indicated.